How To WIN
When the Roof
CaVes In

How To WIN When the Roof CaVes In

BILL GLASS

Fleming H. Revell
Old Tappan, New Jersey

DEDICATION
TO Mavis, my wife, who has suffered
through many roofs caving in and won.
She tempers my quick-fix solutions by forcing
me to a biblical but realistic view.

CONTENTS

7

ACKNOWLEDGMENTS

Through listening to my pastor's messages—occasionally in person and on tape when I'm speaking elsewhere—I got the inspiration for this book. Dickson Rial has a wonderful understanding of how to win when the roof caves in, and he started out being my coauthor. As it developed, this pastor of one of the largest churches in the Dallas area became too busy to have the time to write, so we simply settled for my writing it. Though I also found help from a number of other sources, it is fair to say many of my best ideas were borrowed from Dickson and tried out in my life before they appeared in these pages.

My appreciation to my hard-working typist, Patty Hullett, my mentor, Fred Smith, and other authors who have helped in this book.

My ultimate thanks to Mavis, my wife and partner in suffering, who has taught me more than all the books I've read. I have watched her, close up, go through much pain with her back. She has endured seven major surgeries and unremitting back pain for twenty years, a grandson with Down's syndrome, and numerous other major and minor roofs caving in.

FOREWORD

I have known Bill Glass for many years. First I watched him play football at Baylor and for the Cleveland Browns. Then it was my privilege to be a student along with him in seminary, where we became close friends. Since that time I have kept up with his citywide crusades (which he has conducted for two decades, all over the world), his prison ministry (which has touched thousands of lives), and the eight books he has penned.

Now I am privileged to be his pastor, and as he has written this book, I have shared many of my ideas with him. Over the last ten to fifteen years, in both our lives, God has emphasized the concepts he shares here. We had to write this, because knowing and applying these principles changed our lives.

Dr. John R. W. Stott said it is very easy to be faithful, if you do not care about being contemporary, and it is also easy to be contemporary, if you do not bother to be faithful. Few men of God on the scene today can strike the rare equilibrium of being both, the way Bill can. He is a contemporary, faithful communicator of God's Word. In addition, the material he presents here has been tested—it's not just some theory he has dreamed up. This is real stuff that works where the rubber meets the road.

In these pages you will find the message of robust and victorious living, set within the context of the dramatic document of Holy Scripture. Unlike many preachers—even some *good* ones—Bill Glass has a grasp on the wholeness of the message of the New Testament and of the previews of that message in the Old Testament. The sheer bigness of the gospel blows through his heart and soul. Instead of advising the unconverted to simply "trust Christ" and saying to the struggling, often frustrated Christian, "Try harder, pray more, strive onward, give yourself time," Bill offers the ultimate, often missing answer we all need in such situations: the person of the Holy Spirit.

One day a little boy asked his mother if she knew what Goliath said when David hit him with the stone.

"Why, I didn't know Goliath said anything," she replied.

The boy nodded and said, "When David put that stone in his sling, he whipped it around and let it go. As it hit ol' Goliath right between the eyes, Goliath said, 'Nothing like that has ever entered my mind before.'"

This book aims to offer you some ideas that may never have entered your mind before and to help you put into practice some you've known but never applied. By drawing you nearer to God and helping you understand the spiritual principles involved in facing times of troubles, these words can have a powerful, positive impact on your life.

Let me challenge you to follow them carefully, because they will help you look up into the face of God. If you are hurting, God can help. He wants you to be victorious, even in the middle of your storms. As Bill shares in this volume: "You can win when the roof caves in." Let that truth liberate you!

DICKSON RIAL

INTRODUCTION

In one way or another—to varying degrees, in each of our lives—we've had the roof cave in. As children we discovered that life didn't always run smoothly or go just as we expected, whether it meant losing a big game, falling down and scraping our knees, or having a friend suddenly turn into an enemy.

As time went on and we grew up, we discovered that sometimes the roof that caved in seemed bigger: Suddenly it was not the big game, but our lifework that stood in jeopardy. We no longer had to worry about scraped knees, but physical ailments suddenly threatened to permanently rearrange our lives, or the spouse who was once a best friend became someone with whom we had nothing in common.

When all the roofs begin to cave in, we often start to ask, "Why?" *Have I done something wrong, and is God punishing me? If not, why would He let this happen to me?* We'd like to feel that God will only provide us with the smooth road, the easy way, and the happy life that looks like something out of a picture book. When all that seems to come into question, we doubt our faith, our beliefs, and often God Himself.

Though I may not be able to answer all the *whys*, such situations have a few common elements. When life seems all awry, how we handle them may cause harmony or discord in our lives. I call them the ABCs of winning when the roof caves in:

A. *Event.* When suffering or trouble comes, it usually begins as an event, a specific happening that starts it all. Elisabeth

Elliot, whose husband was killed, along with four other missionaries who were trying to take the gospel to a South American Indian tribe, says, "I think you describe it [my feelings] when you simply say, 'Oh, no!' "

Your child dies, your marriage falls apart, or your reputation is destroyed. Whatever the event, you've had some kind of "oh, no" experience.

B. *Perception.* Now that you've had to face the problem, how do you perceive it? Like most normal people, you may deal with it in a practical way, trying to cope the best you can. But I'd like to propose that you do so in a totally unique, supernatural way! (Don't let this throw you—it really works!)

C. *Response.* How you react to the situation will depend on your perception. If you have a pagan perception, you won't be able to respond in a Christian way. Do you perceive God as a dirty bully, who has it in for you? Or do you see Him as a loving, all-wise Father, who knows and does what is best for you, even though it may not appear so?

Many Christians feel that when you are "Spirit filled," you have automatic responses that simply grow out of the Christian nature. I don't agree. Instead, I believe it is still necessary for the Spirit-filled believer to apply God's principles, through His power. In my own experience, I've discovered that no matter how close I am to the Lord, I still have to reaffirm or claim certain principles.

Now it's time to take a look at these ABCs and the principles that work in each of them.

How To
WIN
When the Roof
CaVes In

PART I

EVENT!

We've all had events in our lives that caused suffering, but when I began to write *How to Win When the Roof Caves In,* the person whose story came to my mind most graphically was that of Mariana Brierton, a woman whom I had met on a preaching mission. Through the years, she has written me, requesting prayer and frankly sharing her problems. Because the extent of her suffering and faith so overwhelmed me, when I began this book, I asked her to write a letter telling about her experiences and thoughts. She replied:

Please don't misunderstand. I did *not* say that God can't or won't work in and through whatever comes our way. Certainly He can and *absolutely He does!* But I have been almost wiped out mentally and emotionally at times in the past when someone conveyed to me the idea, "Well, these things must mean you're not living right," "God must be punishing you for something," and that kind of junk. I was born with brittle bones that snapped and broke in two grinding automobile wrecks. I had polio, which invaded my central nervous system and resulted in my being hospitalized three times, leaving me an eighty-five-pound, morphine-addicted *mess.* When I came home, the doctors told me it would be a "long recovery" (it was!). In the wrecks I had more than fifty bones broken. Many of them were set crooked and had to be rebroken and secured by pins and plates. I lost most of my hearing (95 percent in one ear, 65 percent in the other). In 1973 I was diagnosed as having a debilitating disease that caused me to have to go through two extremely difficult surgeries. Unfortunately, it took my being almost an invalid, requiring bed rest and removal of a lump on a shoulder blade, to find out what it was! After twice thinking it was malignant, the Army Specialization Center in Washington, D.C., made the correct diagnosis of systemic lupus.

I was so fortunate to have Floyd [her husband] and my mom, two very long-suffering people, who stood by me and took care of me and listened to me screaming more than once! I can guarantee you there have been times when they didn't know what to do *with* me or *for* me!

Well, didn't we *pray*, for goodness' sake? Certainly we did!

But even after all Mariana has suffered, she still seems to feel that her suffering is nothing compared to others'. She stated in one of her letters:

Tom Dooley said that he had seen many people in pain, dying, and so on, during his practice as a doctor. Then he went to Vietnam and saw people in dirt-floor huts, alone, cold, with no medical help available. These people didn't have anyone to put cloths on their heads, whisper a comforting word, or clean them up—there wasn't even any soap. He realized that before he had only seen people who, though they indeed were suffering, had the very best care that doctors and nurses could give. That comparison made a lasting impression on me, when I read it in the early sixties, and I *did* always try to remember that no matter what I might be going through, I had wonderful, compassionate doctors, devoted parents and friends, and later, a dear husband who was constantly there (never complaining) to encourage me and help me in every way he knew how. I sometimes wonder how many people do appreciate just what the "white-sheet suffering" means. Always someone to keep you clean and sweet smelling and be there to care—what a blessing!

Then there is a suffering that I know nothing about and cannot even comprehend . . . being rejected and exploited by abusive and cruel parents or spouses. You read so many heartrending things along those lines, and I never cease to be amazed that many of them live through it and come out as whole people, when they find the love of God. He is truly a God of the impossible!

She goes on to say:

There are also the amazing testimonies of those precious and faithful people in other parts of the world who are part of the Suffering Church, imprisoned and tortured and inhumanely treated for their faith in Jesus Christ. How we ought to remember to pray for them every day. Again, I cannot even begin to imagine what such horror would be like.

She concludes by saying:

So I conclude that I know *nothing* about suffering. I have only been through a few difficult circumstances, with much help from all those around me. I've had a very patient and understanding Lord! I've always been very much blessed to have known such a loving family. I've enjoyed Floyd, who has been so strong and loyal all these years, when he so often had a "patient" instead of a wife. I couldn't even give him children (that is a real wound in my spirit). God is so good. Oh, how He loves us and continually draws us closer to Him!

I have received scores of letters from this woman, over a twenty-year period, and she always seems to think that other people have it tougher than she and that the Lord is blessing her and giving her victory. But the truth is that she has to be at the head of the list of the "white-sheet sufferers." As she states, though, there are people who suffer in many different ways, and their suffering seems to be worse than hers—at least in her mind.

What a beautiful spirit this woman has had in the midst of all her agony, and what a profound influence her perception has had on her response! Because she has acknowledged that God isn't out to get her and that there may be something more to the situation than endless, grinding pain, she has been able to achieve a victory over it.

Would you like to know how you can share that?

ONE

REMODELING OUR INADEQUATE ROOMS

When it happens to someone else, you can look at an "oh, no" experience, shake your head sadly, and walk away from it. Or you might try to rationalize God's purpose and debate how Romans 8:28 can be accomplished through it, but still you'll analyze the whole catastrophe at a distance.

However, when it strikes home, it's different, as my wife, Mavis, found in an "oh, no" experience we had in our family. You'll be able to follow her thoughts and the entire situation through these entries she made in her diary.

May 11

Billy Ray was born today, a week early, but we are overjoyed. It has seemed that the nine months it takes to grow a baby has been ten years—we are so excited! Everyone was there to welcome him into the world— Billy (my son, and the father of Billy Ray), Bill (my

23

husband), Bobby (my second son), Mindy (my daughter), Montie (my mother-in-law), the Reynolds (the
other grandparents), and me. He looks perfect to
me—fat, blond, red, but perfect.

May 12

Today the doctors drew Billy aside to tell him the
terrible news—Down's syndrome. I didn't know what
to do but stare in disbelief . . . this can't happen . . .
Laura (my daughter-in-law) hasn't even taken an aspi-
rin during the entire nine months. (Later in the day the
doctors said that couldn't have had any bearing on his
problem. It was simply a "genetic accident.")

I am devastated. I can't think straight. Why? Why?
Why? In one second, I've seen total joy and happiness
disintegrate into the deepest sorrow. Billy Ray has
Down's syndrome. The doctors have been very nice as
they have patiently explained it all to us. They've told
Billy that many parents choose not to see these babies,
they just "put them away" into state or private institu-
tions. They also say that Billy Ray is not "out of the
woods" physically and that many of these babies have
serious heart defects and other internal problems. His
coloring *is* really bad.

My mind is reeling. Why? What did I do wrong?
*Maybe I didn't pray enough—maybe I'm being punished for
something.* Immediately I thought of my *real* concern—
Billy and Laura. How can they stand this?

This baby was going to be perfect—smart and a
football player like his dad and grandad. That is all
impossible. The baby we expected is dead. In his place,
we have a beautiful, blond, fat, red baby (who still

looks great to me). What could we expect now? Fat, healthy babies are one thing—everyone loves babies —but teenagers and adults who have mental retardation and look "different" are another.

Months passed, and I was aware that Mavis struggled. She seemed unusually depressed at times, grasping for answers, questioning, angry at me. She even blamed God. She was hurting and struggling, but her diary reveals some evolution in her thinking.

August 16

The major problem has surfaced: *God*. It's God's fault. I prayed *every* day since Laura first found out she was pregnant. I prayed for two things: for Laura to have an easy time and for a perfect baby. I got two nos and *I am mad*. I have never gotten such distinct *no* answers to prayer—and about something *so* important. Why?

I won't pray anymore. *God has betrayed me,* so forget Him. For three months I've stumbled through my daily tasks, blocking out any thought of God or why this happened. I've tried to talk to Bill about it, and he keeps saying, "Billy Ray is exactly what God wants us to have. He's perfect." I guess he's right, but I'm still mad.

I am seeing real joy and love in Billy and Laura. I'm glad they're okay. God is working in their lives.

I went to the bookstore today—I really need help. (I can't read the Bible.) I found a book called *When Bad Things Happen to Good People*. It's helping some—I can see that someone else has been hurt badly and came through it okay. I don't agree with all his conclusions, but it's comforting to know that someone else struggles out loud.

I honestly feel I'll never be able to smile again. This hurts so badly. When Billy Ray was born, my first concern was for Laura: How would she react? Of course, she was crushed, but ten minutes after Billy told her the problem, she said, *"Bring me my baby."* Billy was hurt to his very innards, but his concern was for *Laura*. I never see Bill cry; I guess he feels he has to stay strong. (Later Bobby told me Bill broke down with him and Billy.) Bobby is growing protective. "He's ours. We'll love him and take care of him." Mindy is hurt for Laura and Billy. Montie is in shock. I remember the first few nights after Billy Ray was born, hearing Billy cry in his bed, trying to sort out his feelings.

I don't know why this has happened. Maybe our family is too proud—proud that we can do just about anything we want to do. Bill and the boys are excellent athletes—the best. Everyone in the family is bright and good-looking—we are sincere Christians and we've taught the kids that they are wonderful in every way, but maybe we've put too much emphasis on their outward abilities. Everyone had been so successful athletically. I have been awfully proud of them. [Billy had played a year of pro ball with Cincinnati, his pro career cut short by injury; Bobby had just come from a tremendous junior year at tackle for Baylor University; Mindy had been cheerleader, basketball star, and runner.]

So here we are with this precious baby boy who can't be all we expected. . . .

As I read her diary, I wish I could have helped her more. The reason I couldn't was because I really didn't understand some of the things that I later learned and have written in this book. However, maybe it's better that she struggled to her own conclusions, because her growth was becoming obvious as I read more.

December 10

We are in the process of tearing out an inferior bathroom to install a good, workable one. All this mess, dust, nails on the floor, open doors (air conditioning getting out and flies getting in), people being here all the time. It's getting to me! I'm wondering why I allowed them to start it in the first place.

Today it dawned on me that the same thing happens to us spiritually. Life is going along pretty well. We may not be as grateful as we should be, or we may be on the bottom spiritually, but somehow we drag along, feeling so-so.

Then God does a remodeling job on us. This can come in the form of sickness, loss of a job, a child going off to college, your marriage, your parents, your family, or as it was in our case, the birth of a grandchild with a problem.

Billy Ray has truly been the Glass family's *Angel Unawares* (as Dale Evans expressed in her book by that title). He is such a doll. He has the unique ability to draw love out of people (also has oodles of his own), has taught all of us the valuable lessons of compassion for those who are different, thankfulness for the "little" blessings of life, lessening of critical attitudes, and a much more realistic attitude of how God works.

These three diary entries show Mavis moving from bewilderment, to anger against God, to realization of God's hand at work in our family.

The *Whys* of Suffering

As she began to doubt, many of Mavis's questions reflected an unspoken belief in an orderly universe. Like everyone else, she had beliefs about ultimate issues such as life, death, happiness, God, good, and evil in herself and others. What was happening in her life—the birth of a handicapped child—didn't seem to fit in with these beliefs, and her suffering brought about a remodeling in her life.

In order to solve problems, we all need to have *some* underlying beliefs—and we all have problems with suffering. When we question, "Why do bad things happen to good people?" certain built-in assumptions go with it. For instance:

1. Asking that question implies we believe life has values, that some things are good, and others are bad. Most everyone would rather have a good life than one of struggle. We would prefer good health to sickness, success to failure, and happiness to sorrow.
2. It assumes order exists in the universe, because it accepts the idea that "bad" things in people's lives have a cause.
3. It reflects the underlying concept that people are important. In fact few of us care whether bad things happen to rabbits or tulips or whatever. Our greatest concern is people, because we assume they are different from animals or plants.

4. Obviously it also expresses the unspoken thought that life is worth living. If not, why bother to ask such questions? Why not just end it all?

5. Finally, such questioning implies we believe we can find and profit from some answers. We assume that we are rational creatures with minds that work, that the universe around us will offer answers, and that eventually we will learn enough so that we can be encouraged to face the struggles of life.

When you look at these assumptions, it's not hard to understand that "Why do bad things happen to good people?" isn't the question we really want to ask. At some time each of us has wondered: *If I know who I am, why am I here? How do I fit into the scheme of things?* What we mean is *What is the purpose of life?*

Why Suffer?

Recently, a miserable man came in to talk to his minister. "I've lost it all—my business, my money, my land—everything," he cried. "It's gone! I feel like committing suicide."

The minister said, "All?"

"Yes, *all!* There is nothing left!"

The minister took a large yellow pad and drew a line down the middle. On the top of one side of the pad, he wrote ASSETS. On the other side he put LOSSES. "Let me ask you. Did you lose your wife?"

The man answered, "Oh, no. She is closer to me than ever before. She's been very comforting, loving, and understanding. She's even gone out and gotten a very good job."

So the minister wrote the word *wife* on the asset side of the pad.

"Well, did you lose your children?"

The man said, "No, I have two wonderful sons, and they've been more supportive than ever before. In fact, they come by and check on me daily. They've offered to help me in every way possible."

The minister added *children* to the assets column.

Then he said, "As a result of this failure, would you say you are better or less qualified to do your job and to run your business?"

The man said, "Well, I'm more qualified. I've worked in my business for forty years, and I understand what to do and what not to do."

The minister wrote *experience* in the same column.

Pressing the issue, he continued, "Would you say that there is a better business atmosphere today than there was the day you started your business?"

The businessman said, "Well, sure. I started my business just after the Depression, in a very unstable economy. There is a much better business atmosphere now!"

Again the minister wrote in the first column: *opportunity*.

"What about the Lord? Don't you think He still loves you?"

The man admitted, "Oh, I'm sure He does."

The pastor placed *God* in the left-hand column. Then he wrote on the LOSSES side *business* and *money*. Turning the yellow pad around, he pushed it in front of the other man and said, "You're a businessman. You're used to reading balance sheets. Which would you say is more impressive, your assets or losses?"

People today are not the only ones who have wondered about or experienced suffering. The Bible gives us examples of those who have suffered, sometimes a great deal and at great length. What did they discover or show us about the purpose of life?

Take Job, in his day, one of the wealthiest, wisest, most godly, and most famous men in the East. But this man saw his world fall apart rapidly, and he became notorious for the anguish he suffered as he endured losses without a cause. Had Job kept a diary like Mavis's, it could have read:

February 9

My servants came to me today and said, "We have some bad news. You have been raided, and you lost all your sheep and all your cattle and all your farmhands. In fact, you've lost it all. You're bankrupt. There's nothing left."

But Job knew you can only judge your real riches by what you still have after you've subtracted everything money can buy. When he faced his calamity, that once-wealthy man wisely said, "Well, things aren't nearly as important as family, and I still have the greatest family in the world." A few hours later, another messenger brought the catastrophic news, "Master Job, all your sons and daughters have been killed." All ten—seven sons and three daughters—gone!

They had all been together in one house when, for some unknown reason, the roof caved in. The children never knew what hit them, and they didn't suffer—they died quickly. But, oh, how Job suffered. He adored his children.

31

Crushed, weeping, and hurting, Job still said, "Well, at least I still have my wife and friends." However, before the words had left his mouth, Job's wife asked, "Why don't you curse God and die?"

Slowly, one by one, his friends turned on him.

Still trying to regroup, Job said to himself, *Well, I'm still strong, and I have my health and can rebuild. It's not the end of the world.* That was before the boils came, and he began to ache and stink from head to toe. Relief only came as he used a broken piece of pottery to scrape the boils open, so the pus could run out.

Never had a man suffered like Job. Yet how did he respond in the midst of being put down by his friends, deserted by his wife, and losing all his goods and children? This down-and-out saint replied, "Though he slay me, yet will I trust in him . . ." (Job 13:15 KJV). Why? Because he had a handle on his purpose in life: to trust God and serve Him, no matter what.

Not only do we find the story of Job's sufferings in Scripture, we also have accounts of the trials of Jesus and Paul.

Jesus, the ultimate sufferer, experienced:

Insult: When He was on the cross, men mocked, ". . . Well, then, come on down from the cross if you are the Son of God" (Matthew 27:40 TLB).

Rejection: One of the apostles records, "Even in his own land and among his own people . . . he was not accepted" (John 1:11 TLB).

Injury: Jesus was so beaten beyond recognition that the book of Isaiah says He looked like a wild animal. He endured our hell.

Yet He was the Creator of the universe, all-powerful and worshiped by angels!

In 2 Corinthians 11:25–28 Paul outlines some of the emotional shocks he felt and the physical shocks he suffered. Outside the Suffering Church, few modern-day Christians have had to endure such treatment. From being a man of background, education, power, and fame, this apostle became the poorest, sickest, most cursed, seemingly God-forsaken man alive.

Job, Jesus, and Paul all fell from extreme heights, to the most shockingly deep valleys. Yet if you study their lives individually, you discover that none of their sufferings were simply bitter pills to be swallowed—they were vital parts of a whole. Paul's thorn and Christ's cross were the toughest and best parts of their lives on earth. And do people remember Job for his money or success in business? No, they know him for his victory in suffering. As Sheldon Kopp said, "Life can be counted on to provide all the pain that any of us might need." But it can open the door to the most vital parts of our lives.

If these three suffered, can we escape? Don't count on it! Pain seems to be the common denominator in our human existence. Jesus warned us, ". . . Here on earth you will have many trials and sorrows . . ." (John 16:33 TLB). Notice that it doesn't say we *might* suffer trials and sorrows—we *will*. We need not ask *if* we will, but *how* and *when*. Suffering is part of life experience, and avoiding it means detouring the essence of life itself.

We need not ask, "Why do bad things happen to good people?" but, "What happens to good people when bad things happen to them?" If suffering is inevitable, how do we handle it?

PART II

———— • ————

PERCEPTION

James Irwin tells of his fascinating experience on that first, historic trip to the moon. Right after blast-off from Cape Canaveral, he looked back out of the spacecraft window and was amazed at how quickly he could see the entire coastline of Florida in one glance. Soon he could see the whole state of Florida. Then he got a coast-to-coast view of the United States. Before long he could see the curvature of the whole world. Planet Earth quickly began to shrink to the size of a basketball, then a baseball, and finally a golf ball.

When he landed on the moon, Irwin no longer looked back; he looked up. Standing on the surface of the moon, he was thrilled with the panorama that lay before him. Amazingly though, that which was familiar—Earth—impressed him most! He saw our planet from a new perspective, and it seemed mystically beautiful, peaceful, and inviting. Enamored, the astronaut gazed at the Earth, floating against the black backdrop of space like a beautiful, azure marble. He extended his thumb and forefinger above his eyes, framing the world between his fingers, and said, "There are five billion people living on planet Earth, and all of them are between my thumb and forefinger. One malfunction, and I may never return to Earth." For the first time a man could look at the Earth in much the way God does, objectively, unencumbered with the trivia of day-to-day life.

When we experience the A in the ABCs of winning when the roof caves in, we usually don't have a very long-distance view of what is going on in our lives. Wrapped up in the "oh, no" event, we may lose sight of the importance of B—perception. We can begin to see the world as something we have to control and God as someone who has forgotten about us or who doesn't care anymore. If we do that, we simply show our own shortsightedness and foolishness. God alone is wise, strong, and loving enough to cause all things to "work together for good." He is in control, and the world is not an accident. He loves and cares about all of us, and He guides our lives without destroying our accountability.

Just as Jim Irwin got an otherworldly view of the Earth from the moon, we need to see things from a new vantage point. Let's attempt to blast off to a more elevated position. Breaking the bonds of everyday thinking may be tough, but we must do it in order to see things as God wants us to. Often through suffering we become aware of the things that really count.

In later chapters we'll look at how to get that higher view: to ascend to a place where the stink of the Prodigal Son's hog pen, the pus around Paul's thorn, the misery of the cross with its dead Christ, and the thunder of the collapsing roof on the boil-covered back of Job aren't deafening enough to blot out the still, small voice of God.

TWO

YOU CAN'T GROW WITHOUT SUFFERING

If God loves us, how can He build suffering into the whole human experience? Can our compassionate heavenly Father really expect us to go through painful trials?

In Scripture, God compares Himself to an earthly father. "If a child asks his father for a loaf of bread, will he be given a stone instead? If he asks for fish, will he be given a poisonous snake? Of course not!" Jesus affirmed. Then He went on to point out God's infinitely greater abilities, understanding, and perception, with the words, "And if you hardhearted, sinful men know how to give good gifts to your children, won't your Father in heaven even more certainly give good gifts to those who ask him for them?" (Matthew 7:9–11 TLB).

We can count on God's love, but that does not mean we can also count on Him to let us have anything we desire. Like a good parent, He has more care for us than that.

Unlike some human parents, God neither abuses His children nor avoids painful discipline.

The father who abuses his child can scar that boy or girl for life. Perhaps it's as bad as no discipline at all. Seldom will an undisciplined child love his parents. He subconsciously thinks he's not even worth a whipping when he misbehaves.

Nor was the Prodigal Son's father smart in giving his son his inheritance early. All of us have seen children ruined as a result of receiving their inheritance before they matured. On second thought maybe the father knew his son was so bullheaded he would never mature unless he hit bottom. Only after the son had the freedom to end up in the pigpen, eating pig food, could he "come to himself" (see Luke 15:17).

Though God loves and forgives us, we remain properly accountable for our mistakes, and He has made that a part of the system: "Your own wickedness will correct you, And your backslidings will reprove you . . . ," He promises (Jeremiah 2:19 NKJV). Any difficulties that come from God are sent into our lives to express His love: "For whom the Lord loves He chastens . . ." (Hebrews 12:6 NKJV). If you want to raise a fool, take the consequences out of a child's mistakes!

Like the parent who disciplines his child because he loves the boy, God proves His love by giving us indications that we have gotten out of His will. Scripture tells us, "He who spares his rod hates his son . . ." (Proverbs 13:24 NAS). When we get out of line, God lets us know, without abusing us.

God sends us enough adversity to make us examine our inner selves. Anna felt deep feelings of inadequacy and unacceptability. Although she had always looked up to her parents, they had never encouraged her, but always criticized, and she had struggled with feelings of inferiority ever since. When she faced one severe emotional crisis, she began to deal with these inadequacies. As a result, the adversities that caused the crisis enabled Anna to more fully accept God's love.

A Time for Everything

As God provides us with both discipline and love, He shows His understanding of the importance of the rhythm of the two. Sometimes we need more love than discipline; other times we'll need a heavy dose of discipline to bring us closer to Him. Whatever's best, He provides, even if it's not what we'd ask for.

When we go to God for something, our own expectations of what we need to receive and when we need it may get in our way. Remember Christ's miracle at the wedding at Cana? More guests came than the family expected. Our Lord's mother came to Him, saying, "The wine has expired, perform a miracle and keep our friends from shame." Mary knew Jesus could do the unusual: He was virgin born; when He was only twelve, she had heard Him astound the priests in the Temple. She had ". . . kept all these things and pondered them in her heart" (Luke 2:19 NKJV). But Jesus could not be rushed. He told her, "Woman, my hour has not yet come." By this He meant, "Do not rush Me. I am running on schedule. I am going to perform a miracle, but not right now."

Many of us, guilty of Mary's blunder, pray for loved ones and want our prayers answered immediately. Like small children, we want it *now!* If God does not immediately respond the way we want, we become impatient with Him and with life. Instead of rushing, we need to learn how to ". . . run with patience the particular race that God has set before us" (Hebrews 12:1 TLB).

God knows exactly how to pass out His blessing and suffering, to produce character in us. In ignorance, a sick child may look upon parents and doctor as enemies, because they want to give her a shot. How do the parents steel themselves to see their girl suffer? Because they and the doctor know that's the only way she will get well. It's the same way with the all-knowing Father and His children.

Sometimes God has to allow disappointments in our lives, in order to make us succeed:

If Phillips Brooks had succeeded as a schoolmaster, he would never have stood in the pulpit, to move people with his mighty ministry.

Though Frederick Robinson was crushed by his failure to get a commission in the British army, that failure forced him to become a great preacher, who moved congregations by his mighty spirit.

Had Nathaniel Hawthorne been retained at the custom house, he never would have written his wonderful studies in the deep places of human sorrow, love, and sin.

For each of these men, failure in their first professions led to an infinitely more important success. What if these men had given up in despair and jumped from tall buildings as many did in the 1929 stock market crash? They would have missed the whole point of their existence.

•

A Purpose in Suffering

Often, like children who wish to avoid the doctor, we have to be dragged, kicking and screaming, to face up to our suffering. As long as we object, we simply make our pain worse by our resistance. If we could open up to it and see suffering as a friend, we might see God's hand working in the situation.

All encouragement and no discipline results in a spoiled brat who comes in constant conflict with authority. The alternative, too much discipline, is equally unwise. Just as a parent combines discipline with assurances of love, our heavenly Father perfectly mixes joy and sorrow. Problems and pain are as much parts of our growth as victory and health.

Through it all, God promises, "I will strengthen thee" (*see* Isaiah 41:10). The Greek word *strengthen* means "to equip, to toughen, to get you ready." Suffering works to strengthen a professional sports team. Dallas Cowboy coach Tom Landry said, "I make my players do what they don't want to do [training camp and continuous practice] so they can accomplish what they want more than anything [the Super Bowl]." This great coach recognizes that players have to go through the pain of training camp to emerge winners.

Trials Toughen

Though "no pain, no gain" is a football slogan, you can see its truth in Scripture and in the very fabric of the universe. The psalmist recognized it when he said, "Before I was afflicted I went astray, But now I keep Your word. . . . It is good for me that I have been afflicted, That I may learn

Your statutes. . . . I know, O Lord, that Your judgments are right, And that in faithfulness You have afflicted me" (Psalms 119:67, 71, 75 NKJV).

I played twenty-two seasons and lived through twenty-two football training camps! I've heard players gripe. I've agonized with others as we've strained and sweated. I've grown sore, been knocked unconscious, had broken bones, had ligaments stretched, been cut and bleeding. Because I knew it was the only way to get in shape for the season, I suffered through training camp. But as I looked back on it, after winning the championship, the summer of suffering was as nothing, compared to the joy of victory. I had suffered in a good cause. Getting in shape was always painful, but if I didn't suffer, I didn't grow. To make a muscle stronger, you actually must tear it down. There are no miracles involved in preparation for the Super Bowl. It is a daily commitment, and the dailiness of it can get boring and turn into drudgery, if in faith, you don't keep your mind on the big game coming up.

Speaking about winning the game, legendary coach Vince Lombardi described the intensity it requires:

> Every time a football player goes out to play, he's got to play from the ground up. From the soles of his feet right up to his head. Every inch of him has to play. Some guys play with their heads. That's OK—you've got to be smart to be number one in any business, but in football, you've got to play with your heart. With every fiber of your body. If you are lucky enough to find a guy with a lot of head and a lot of heart, he's never going to come off the field second.

It is a reality of life that men are competitive and the most competitive games draw the most competitive men. That's why they're there—to compete. They know the rules and the objectives when they get in the game. The objective is to win—fairly, squarely, decently, by the rules—but to win. And in truth, I have never known a man worth his salt who in the long run, deep down in his heart, did not appreciate the grind—the discipline. There is something in good men that really yearns for . . . needs . . . discipline and the harsh reality of head-to-head combat.

I don't say these things because I believe in the "brute" nature of man or that man must be brutalized to be combative. I believe in God and I believe in human decency. But I firmly believe that any man's finest hour, his greatest fulfillment to all he holds dear, is the moment when he has worked his heart out in a good cause and lies exhausted on the field of battle, victorious.

Lombardi catches the spirit of "head-to-head combat" when he describes his hero as prostrate on the field of battle, after pouring his all into the game. He now lies exhausted, fulfilled, experiencing his finest hour, victorious. But the ultimate win came only after many toughening hours of preparation.

That coach also picked up the key of suffering when he said pain is not just necessary, but should be welcomed as a friend: "There is something in good men that really yearns for . . . needs . . . discipline and the harsh reality of head-to-head combat." I'm sure many men who played the game didn't understand. They stuck it out because they feared the coach, but some of us ultimately came to see this truth clearly.

Entering the war. Suffering is a battle, and soldiers know all about it. When they experience warfare, they expect hardships. In his address to Martis, Tertullian wrote, "No soldier comes to war surrounded by luxuries, nor goes into action from a comfortable bedroom, but from the makeshift and narrow tent where every kind of hardness and unpleasantness is to be found."

During wartime, even people who are not soldiers will suffer much in a good cause. During World War II, if you were doing something that seemed a little extravagant, others would say, "How can you do that? There is a war on!" Restrictions and warfare go hand in hand.

There is no such thing as cheap victory: It costs a lot of pain and suffering, and you won't find it at the end of a rainbow or atop the ladder of success. Victory's price tag reads *faithfulness, endurance,* and always *sorrow.* Wisdom will teach us that the winner's cup can only be as deep as our cup of sorrow.

Later in life this truth fully dawned on me. After Billy Ray—or maybe it was my son Bobby's divorce or several other problems I had—I began to see "through a glass, darkly" (1 Corinthians 13:12 KJV). Just as a coach pushed me to greater effort in training camp, God toughens me up for the game. Whether or not the players understand the necessity for drills, the coach makes them endure the pain. Occasionally God has to do the same with us. C. H. Spurgeon pointed out the meaning behind God's method when he said, "The important thing about a problem is not the solution, but the strength we gain in finding the solution."

Those who have suffered. When we suffer, we need to look at others who have also done so, and take heart. Shepherd boy David often faced hardship while protecting his sheep. Occasionally he faced a bear or lion and had to kill the beast that threatened his flock. In addition David slept among the rocks, ate wild game, and so on. What was God doing? He was equipping, teaching, and toughening the man who would one day have to face Goliath. Someday you, too, may have a giant to fight.

As you look at people in the Bible, consider the apostle Paul, who received a strange gift from God. Paul says he was given ". . . a thorn in the flesh, the messenger of Satan to buffet me . . ." (2 Corinthians 12:7 KJV). *Buffet* means "taking your fists and beating someone repeatedly." So Paul's saying, "God gave me a suffering that pounded me."

When Paul said "there was given to me a thorn," his words mean he was nailed to the floor. This wasn't something from a delicate rosebush, but a huge nail, like the spikes they used for crucifying. Paul couldn't move. He was stuck. That thorn had control of him.

What exactly was the thorn? We don't know. But I'm glad Paul didn't tell us, because his figurative use of the word lets it fit all kinds of situations. You can compare any physical, emotional, or spiritual problem that has you "nailed to the floor" to Paul's thorn.

How did Paul respond to this gift? "I have asked the Lord thrice that it might depart from me . . . ," he said (*see* v. 8). *Thrice* could actually mean he asked God many times.

In verse 9 he tells us God's response: ". . . And he said

unto me the same thing that he did the first time I asked."
God never wavered. He said no that first time, and He said
no the second, and no every other time Paul asked. But He
also said, "Paul, if I don't make you weak, then I can't make
you strong."

What else does Paul know about troubles? In 2 Corinthians 11:24 he says he took thirty-nine stripes. He's not
talking about a little switch Mama picked off a tree, to use to
spank Junior. He means a cat-o'-nine-tails, a whip made out
of nine pieces of leather, with a chunk of bone tied to the
end of each strip. Strong men died from this kind of
punishment.

Paul had gone through this ordeal *five* times! In addition
he suffered three beatings with a rod, one stoning, three
shipwrecks, no food, no clothes, and not many friends. He
certainly earned the right to call himself our fellow sufferer.
Still, he "pressed toward the mark," rejoiced through
beatings, stonings, shipwrecks, and all. What happened?
People began to say, "It can't be Paul—look at that pitiful
mess—it has to be God's supernatural intervention that
makes him able to go through this!"

Did God just have some special method He used only on
Paul? Not really. He's tested and improved many saints by
suffering. Take a look at Moses. God said, "I want you to
lead My people out of Egypt." But Moses fumbled the ball
when he murdered the Egyptian, and God put him on the
bench, on his backside, in the back side of the desert. Moses
learned about suffering.

After forty years in the desert, God finally said, "Moses, I
think you're ready." Did Moses sound thrilled at the idea of
working for God again? No, he answered, "I'm not ready,

Lord. I have no ability; I have no authority. They won't listen to me. You benched me forty years ago, because I was such a failure. I can't even speak."

Once He heard that, God told Moses, "Now you are ready. Now you are weak enough that I can use you."

Forty years ago Moses had said, "I can do it, Lord. I can do it!" God showed him, "I can't use you this way."

Once Moses could say, "I can't do it, there is no way. You had better get somebody else," the suffering had done what God planned.

Your thorn has been given to you for your good, even if you do not understand it. "It doesn't feel good," you may say. Do you think Paul's thorn felt good? Of course not. If it had, he wouldn't have prayed for God to take it away. But God told Paul, "I am giving you this gift because it will make you weak, and that will make you strong in Me."

God often works in opposites. He may say:

"I'll make you weak, so you can be strong."

"I'll let you suffer, so you can have victory."

"I'll make it hard on you here, so you can appreciate heaven."

"I'll make you poor, so you can have real riches."

When you are weak or suffering, God can begin to reach you. He can start to show you what He has in mind, once He has your attention!

THREE

WHAT'S GOD UP TO?

Lord, I'm in this mess. I need wisdom. You said ask, so I'm asking." When he has a problem, my pastor often prays this way, taking literally James 1:5 (NAS), "But if any of you lacks wisdom, let him ask of God. . . ."

"One time when I was struggling with a problem, I remembered this verse and decided to claim it. Since that time," he recalls, "anytime and in any situation, when I say, 'Lord, I need wisdom about this problem or need,' He gives me an impression in my heart. Whenever I follow it, everything always works out right."

If you are puzzled by your problem and can't figure out what God is up to in your life, just ask for His wisdom. He'll give you impressions about what to do, and you can be certain of His leading. Though you may be able to misinterpret His will, when you claim God's wisdom and receive a clear, lasting impression consistent with the Bible, you can act in faith.

One famous Christian, George Mueller, described the steps he used in discovering God's will:

> I seek at the beginning to get my heart into such a state that it has no will of its own in regard to a given matter. Having done this, I do not leave the result to feeling or simple impression. If I do so, I make myself liable to great delusions. I seek the will of the Spirit of God through, or in connection with, the Word of God. . . . Thus, through prayer to God, the study of the Word and reflection, I come to a deliberate judgment according to the best of my ability and knowledge, and if my mind is thus at peace, and continues so after two or three more petitions, I proceed accordingly. In trivial matters, and in transactions involving more important issues, I have found this method always effective.

The God Who Is Enough

What if we *have* sought God's will, and life just seems to get tougher? Is it so hard to believe that God is working in our lives, even when we suffer? Like the little boy who mistakenly sang the hymn "Trust and Obey" as "Trust and Okay," we need to get the idea that everything *is* okay, because God runs the universe.

> *Tis far, far better to let Him choose,*
> *The way we should take;*
> *If only we leave our lives to Him,*
> *He will guide without mistake.*
>
> *We, in our blindness, would never choose,*
> *A pathway dark and rough,*

52

And so we should ever find in Him,
"The God who is enough."

No matter what happens to us in life, God is still and always enough. Nothing is out of His hands.

A radio announcer once asked Leo Durocher, manager of the New York Giants, "Barring the unforeseen, Leo, will your club get the pennant?" Durocher responded, "There ain't going to be no unforeseen." Even less, can there be any unforeseen for God; we can know that, whatever happens, He has it all under control.

Shaken Into Awareness

If you get into a poor life-style and can't get out of that rut, God may send a crisis. His purpose? After you've been knocked flat on your back and have to look up, you can see His *enough.*

Frozen into his Pharisaism, Saul became obsessed with the desire to destroy all Christians. Like most Pharisees he actually believed that ridding the earth of all unbelieving Jews would somehow cause the Messiah to come.

As Stephen died a painful death from stoning, Saul heard him pray, "Father, forgive them, for they know not what they do," but the Pharisee still didn't get the message. Though he had seen that wonderful deacon die so unselfishly, had seen the evidence for the Resurrection, and had heard of all the miracles of Jesus, Saul still wasn't paying much attention to God. He saw Christians die by the thousands for their faith, but he still felt determined to destroy them.

Only after God struck him blind on the road to Damascus

did Saul begin to pay attention to Him. Before the man who was to become the apostle Paul could look to God for help, he had to be flattened by a divine laser beam.

Sometimes it's the same with us: God may give us a kick in the pants to get our attention.

Maybe your child starts giving trouble at school, and you fail to deal with the issue. As long as you avoid them, the problems multiply in number and intensity. Soon the little girl you've ignored begins to think she'll run away from home as soon as she gets the chance. Because you haven't spent time with her and shown her you value her, she thinks she'll find love somewhere else. On the day she disappears, you finally realize that you have a *big* problem.

When small reminders don't turn us to God's way, He also lets things snowball. It's all part of His plan to wipe out the things that keep us from giving Him first place. When the small nudges don't make us remove what's in that spot, He'll give us a real attention getter!

In the Sermon on the Mount, Jesus told of two people. One built a house on the rock, the other built on sand. The same wind blew against each house—both were tested equally. Like those houses, people can stand or fall, depending on their foundations. Adversity tests our works.

God doesn't test you to find out if you'll stand, because He doesn't need that information. He knows what you'll do before you do it. Nor is He like a teacher who gives you problems to work, to test what you know; instead He matures you through this process.

However, God doesn't only give you the trials; He combines discipline and blessing in a proper balance.

In working with inmates in my prison ministry, I have

discovered that the life of a child who becomes a criminal lacks discipline and blessing, and these missing elements cause maladjustment. Criminologists agree that it starts early, and the criminal mind is apparent by the third grade. With some consistency they can pick out future criminals at this age.

Thank God that He doesn't leave these key ingredients out of our lives. He mixes them, to help us mature. As we do, we must learn the Christian response to trials, knowing He works in both the spanking and the blessing.

What Causes Suffering?

You may say, "All that might be true, but isn't some of our suffering caused by Satan?" Yes, however, Scripture says, "Even that which Satan intends for evil, God can use for good" (see Genesis 50:20). In other words, God can actually turn the tables on the devil!

The "evil one" intended to destroy Joseph by all the adversity that was thrown at him. Joseph's brothers sold him into slavery; he was lied about and thrown into prison and forgotten in that dark dungeon. What tragedy! Yet God turned all this into good. Joseph saved Egypt and his own family from starvation and became a beautiful picture of Christ, because of his victory over problems.

What About Sin?

Someone else may ask, "But can't sin cause suffering, too?" Maybe so, but it also can work together for our good. Though David suffered repeatedly because of his own sin, God used that to mature David.

Satan whispers in your ear, "How can you believe God is

at work, when obviously it is Satan?" Or maybe he attacks you with, "You have to take responsibility for this yourself. It was your own sin." In other words, the evil one is saying, "In situations where you've done wrong, you're on your own, partner."

This is the very time you need God most! Ask Him to forgive you and start to work it out. Often you may feel so guilty, because of your sin, that you want to be punished. You feel you must suffer and somehow pay for it. But this kind of masochism denies God's grace; it "tramples the blood of Christ beneath our feet" (*see* Hebrews 10:29).

Disaster may have come into your life because of sin. When you are guilty, ask for forgiveness and believe God has given you a second chance. Saying you are forgiven, yet continuing to punish yourself with guilt is a lack of faith. And don't take the blame when you *aren't* responsible— that's mentally unhealthy.

God's Signature

"But if any of you lacks wisdom, let him *ask* of God . . ." (James 1:5 NAS). When you face your trials and sufferings and look with this kind of wisdom, to your amazement, you will find God's signature on everything that touches your life:

> Though your gross sin could never be of God, you'll begin to
> see how He uses it to mold you into His image.
> Though others have done evil to you, you'll eventually find
> ways in which those things you hate have helped you.
> Though you have experienced many physical pains, you'll
> see you've had some subtle benefits, too.

Without exception, your first reaction to suffering should be one of faith. "I don't know how this could possibly 'work together for good,' but I'm certain it shall," is a prayer of faith. Don't start questioning God, just pray for wisdom. Then wait expectantly to see His autograph—not on the sin, but on its being worked out. If you feel yourself wavering, continue to reclaim this promise of God's working in your life.

Sometimes you will understand everything in a sudden flash of insight, but more often, comprehension comes with time. Looking back at your tragedy, you discover that in it, God actually entered history again. Though Jesus did not visit the planet in a physical sense, you saw divine intervention.

True, in some cases God never in this life reveals how He is involved, and in those incomprehensible calamities we are pushed back on faith. In heaven we will know, but we only see ". . . now, as if we were peering at his reflection in a poor mirror . . ." (1 Corinthians 13:12 TLB).

We have such a dim view of life. Why is the glass through which we look so dark? Perhaps because the God who made us is on a different level from us intellectually, methodically, and in His way of recording time.

God Is Pure Intellect

"This plan of mine is not what you would work out, neither are my thoughts the same as yours! For just as the heavens are higher than the earth, so are my ways higher than yours, and my thoughts than yours" (Isaiah 55:8, 9 TLB). God is pure intellect, and He has perfect knowledge, including advance knowledge of what will happen. We, victims of partial understanding, are prone to make mistakes and view life with tunnel vision. But God sees the beginning, end, and everything between them. "For the wisdom of this world is foolishness to God. As it says in the book of Job, God uses man's own brilliance to trap him; he stumbles over his own 'wisdom' and falls" (1 Corinthians 3:19 TLB).

Watching a parade from street level, you can only see one float going by at a time. A person sitting on a high building not only sees what the street-level viewer does, but can also look at the beginning and finish of the parade. In your life, it's as if you were watching from street level, while God was sitting above, viewing the whole. He knows how the present problem fits into your life. His pure intellect combines with "infinite" wisdom as He works out your life.

God Uses Perfect Methods

Not only does He accomplish His methods through perfect wisdom, God also does it in a perfect way. "For as the heavens are higher than the earth, So are My ways higher than your ways . . ." (Isaiah 55:9 NAS).

A baby may play with something dangerous, like matches. When the mother takes them away, the child cries and thinks Mother is mean. She doesn't understand that her mother is keeping her from hurting herself. In the same way, God sees some things we are doing and takes them away because He can see the pain that will come if we continue.

Because He works on a higher plane, we may have a hard time comprehending God's ways. Often we misunderstand His moves, because we are victims of time and space.

When the children of Israel stumbled through the desert, snakes came and began to bite and kill the people. Everyone felt frightened.

God told Moses to sculpt a brass serpent and place it on a pole. "If your people look up, they will live," God promised. He did not say, "Moses, organize a society for the extermination of snakes." Many of his people must have argued, "Who ever heard of looking at a brass snake for a problem like this?" They were the ones who died, because they could not understand that God was working on a different level.

We can see God's perfect method in creation. The winding, snakelike river, the jagged coast, the ever-changing sea, the billowing clouds, the bulging mountains all seem so haphazard, but to change any of them, even in a minor way, can cause unparalleled damage. Acid rain, ozone-layer thinning, and other environmental damage proves creation's delicate balance.

Comparing the beauty of the natural world with man-made structures reminds us that only God creates. Man manufactures, using creation's raw materials. God creates from nothing (*ex nihilo*). Seldom does His beauty resemble man's buildings, with their crude, straight lines, square shapes, or circular designs. He builds trees with every leaf and limb different and beautiful. All the stresses and strains of the tree are recorded in its rings.

When it comes to creation, we human beings tend to label some things *bad* that might not be that at all. If it isn't to *our* liking, though, we call it a curse and feel it should be eliminated or that God should supernaturally change it.

If we cut down on the wolf population, rabbits take over. When the rabbits multiply without check, they eat too much grass, which causes starvation and death for many other animals. Now our "good" change looks a little different, doesn't it?

An Eskimo would call blubber the most essential thing in the world—and to him, it is, because he kills the whale and uses its fat as a staple of his diet. We can't imagine sitting down to a bowl of blubber. Can you see Jane Fonda eating it? Though we avoid fat in our diets, the Eskimo needs it to keep him from dying in the Arctic cold. Blubber is imperative to his health.

Likewise, what we look at as evil suffering, from God's perspective, might not be bad at all. But that still doesn't solve many difficult questions, such as, "How can it be good for millions of innocent children to die of starvation?" or, "How could it be good for innocent victims to die in excruciating ways?" Only God knows.

God Counts Time Differently

Second Peter 3:8 reminds us that to God a thousand years are as one day. To us, a thousand years are a long time— seventy years seems a lot to us—but to God, time is different. According to His arithmetic, if a thousand years are like one day, then forty years are about one hour. That means if you live eighty years, as far as God is concerned, you have only lived roughly two hours.

Who's in Control?

In one of his books, Robert Louis Stevenson tells of a sailing vessel heading toward the coast of New England. A storm came up, and the boat was dangerously close to the shoreline. Fearing a shipwreck, the passengers sent a man up to talk to the captain. When the passengers' representative walked in to the control room, the captain turned and gave the man a broad smile, then once again focused on steering the vessel away from the rocks. When the representative returned to the passengers, they asked, "What did the captain say?" He replied, "He didn't have to say a word. He has his hands on the wheel. He's in control of the vessel. And he turned to me and smiled, and his smile said that everything is well."

The Captain of our faith has His hands on our destiny. His smiling face is looking down on us. As we look to Him, He assures us that He is with us.

Since God is with us, what are we worrying about?

FOUR

ALL
DOESN'T MEAN
"MOST"

I don't believe the age of miracles has passed. But God doesn't automatically use them, because we tend to grow more in the struggle against a problem than in the comfort of enjoying a great blessing. Still, a lot of spoiled-brat Christians want to be treated to "good" miracles, and avoid the "bad" thorns.

What's Good?

We can't really define *good* and *bad* in those simplistic terms. Though I may think something is "bad" today, five or ten years from now, I might discover it was "good." Worse, when I begin to think that I can define *good* and *bad* in circumstances, I also tend to define people in the same terms. "Those who agree with me" are *good,* and "those who disagree with me" are *bad.*

An old Chinese story tells of a man who bought his son a pony for his birthday. All his friends came to the birthday party, and they said, "It's good that you bought your son such a beautiful pony." The man said, "Who knows? It may be good and it may be bad." When the pony ran away, everybody said, "That's bad that the pony ran away." The man said, "Who knows?" The pony came back and brought twelve wild ponies with him. Everybody said, "That's good." He said, "Who knows?" As he tried to break one of the wild ponies, the boy was thrown off and broke his leg. Again they said, "That's bad." The man said, "Who knows?" A ruler came through the territory, soliciting troops for a war that was raging, and the son couldn't serve in the army because of his broken leg. Everybody said, "That's good." The man said, "Who knows?"

It's always difficult to define good and bad. But we also have another problem when we try to label things this way: Scripture says that for Christians God causes ". . . all things [to] work together for good . . ." (Romans 8:28 KJV). So even if we can define an event as intrinsically evil, good can still come out of it.

Often after a spouse's death, the remaining loved one appears to handle the situation beautifully. Usually he is actually in shock. Though he handles the funeral and its aftermath well, later the grief process begins to take its toll, reality sets in, and the loss becomes apparent. Nothing seems good. That's when he needs to exercise faith. Everything *is* awful in the present; the only hope is that in some wonderful, unseen way, God is, in fact, at work!

"And we know that all things work together for good. . . ." Emphasize that word *know!* The Greek word Paul uses there means "we know for certain"! You don't have to wait and see if God is going to come through. F. B. Meyer says, "If any promise of God should fail, heaven would clothe itself with sackcloth. The sun and the moon and the stars would leave their courses. The universe would rock and the hollow wind would groan through a ruined civilization the awful message that God can lie." God will not lie. His own integrity backs this truth. God will make all things "work" together for good, even if the problem is unbelievably awful.

It isn't difficult to see that good will come out of good. But believing that good comes out of bad is where you stretch your faith.

All Means Exactly That

"How can painful, unpleasant, hurtful things work for good?" you ask. Let's look at some examples from Scripture and modern life.

The people of Israel were carried away to Babylon as slaves for seventy years. Knowing how they griped in the desert, on the way to the Promised Land, they must have *really* turned the air blue with curses against God and the Babylonians for taking them away into slavery. "This can't possibly serve any good purpose," they complained, but history proves it was a turning point for the entire nation. These Jews hadn't let the land rest each seventh year, as God commanded. They had disobeyed the sabbath rest of the land for 490 years, so God gave the land its rest all at once—for 70 years. He did all of this "for their good."

"The punishment you gave me was the best thing that could have happened to me, for it taught me to pay attention to your laws . . ." (Psalms 119:71 TLB). The psalmist realized that when troubles came into his life, it was good for him, because he learned something.

God is going to allow some sorrow into your life. If you will listen, He will teach you some things through that. Some people have even had good come through a close brush with death.

Out-of-Body Experiences

All the new life-support technology making it possible to bring people back from the point of death has produced a new phenomenon: There have been thousands of recorded cases of people dying and coming back to life. Many tell of their souls rising out of their bodies and hovering above and entering a long tunnel, at the end of which is a beautiful light. Then they are suddenly snatched back. Because this is such a common experience, I consider it reliable.

There are even reported cases on hell experiences. Dr. Morris Rowling from Chattanooga, Tennessee, tells of trying to save the life of a patient. He was using every technique and procedure that he could think of to battle for the man's life. But as the vital signs would weaken, the man would moan loudly, "I'm going to hell, I'm going to hell. I am leaving my body, and I'm going to hell." After some time he stabilized the patient, but he couldn't get that doleful cry out of his mind—"I'm leaving my body, and I'm going to hell." By studying reports of many patients who had dying experiences, the doctor became something of an authority on people entering their eternal reward and being snatched back to this life.

On a recent TV interview a psychologist explained it away by reasoning, "The patient is simply projecting what he imagines will happen after death." Dr. Rowling protested, "That was what I would have said, because I was an outspoken agnostic. But I made a comprehensive study of this, and I discovered to my amazement that all the experiences were remarkably alike. One would expect that they would be extremely dissimilar, if they were simply imaginary, because everyone's imagination would work differently, therefore conjuring up different daydreams. The second thing that convinced me that these people were actually on the front porch of eternity is more subjective. The patient is always absolutely sure that his experience was real. Third, let's return to a more objective observation. The patients were always surprised as to how different the dying episodes were from what they thought they would be. There was one sentence I heard repeated often: 'Dying is nothing like I thought it would be.' "

Dr. Rowling concluded, "The patient kept passing in and out of life. Everytime his vital signs went down, he shouted, 'I'm leaving my body, and I'm going to hell.' This caused me many a sleepless night. After studying numerous cases objectively, I came to one conclusion. These people *are* actually dying and approaching heaven or hell. I knew where I'd go when I died, and it wasn't heaven. So I trusted Christ!"

This isn't unique to our day. I found some deathbed statements in an old book titled *Shoe-Leather Faith* and noticed they sound like current ones. No one has to tell you which of these are Christians and which are famous atheists:

"The chariot has come, and I am ready to step in."

MARGARET PRIOR

"Eternity rolls up before me like a sea of glory."

JORDAN ANTIE

"How bright the room! How full of angels!"

MARTHA McCRACKIN

"I wish I had the power of writing; I would describe how pleasant it is to die."

DR. CULLEN

"The sun is setting; mine is rising. I go from this bed for a crown. Farewell."

S. B. BANGS

"Can this be death? Why, it is better than living! Tell them I die happy in Jesus."

JOHN ARTHUR LYTH

"I am suffering the pangs of the damned."

TALLYRAND PERIGORD

"Give me laudanum that I may not think of eternity."

MIRABEAU

"I am abandoned by God and man! I shall go to hell! O Christ! O Jesus Christ!"

VOLTAIRE

"What blood, what murders, what evil counsels have I followed! I am lost; I see it well!"

CHARLES IX, KING OF FRANCE

"I would give worlds, if I had them, if the 'Age of Reason' had never been published. O Lord, help me! Christ, help me! Stay with me! It is hell to be left alone!"

TOM PAINE

What's the Use?

Close encounters with death always have a chilling impact on people. It's enough to turn their lives around. But less dramatic experiences may also slap us in the face as God uses them to prod us in the right direction. It's like that Skin Bracer commercial. If you sing out, "I needed that," and take the warning, all is well. But if you continue a course away from God, you will get clobbered in a more convincing way.

It is as if God suits the chastisement (Hebrews 12:6) to the hardness of our heads—not to the depth of our sin. He knows what we need to bring us into line. At first He may send only a little wind into our lives. But if we don't respond, He sends a stronger storm and finally a full-fledged hurricane. Whatever is necessary to get our attention, that He will do.

Obviously all suffering isn't God trying to get our attention, just as it doesn't always result from our sins. But there is usefulness behind all types of suffering, though we seldom immediately understand it.

Genesis 50:20 tells how Joseph had been betrayed by his own brothers. He had been sold as a slave into a strange country, where he had no friends. He was falsely thrown in prison. He was even forgotten in the prison, after others had promised to tell pharaoh about his abilities. Still, Joseph could confront his brothers and say, "You meant evil against me, but God allowed it to happen for good. For it saved a nation."

Manesseh, the king of Israel, was taken away in chains to Assyria (2 Chronicles 33). In summary he says, "It was good that I was forced off my throne. I exchanged my crown for chains. When I was chained, I realized how wrong I had been about God." Manesseh didn't know God was real until he was in chains. Thank God for chains!

For almost twenty years now, I've led a team that conducts a ministry in which we take top pro athletes, representing several different sports, into prisons. We do athletic clinics, discussing and even giving demonstrations about our particular sport; then we briefly share our faith with the inmates. Between thirty and fifty counselors go into each prison with us, and we usually conduct our program in five to ten prisons on the same weekend. So several hundred counselors and around ten pro athletes go with us on each of these three-day encounters. Over 4,000 counselors have served with us through the years. We have been in over 400 of the 600 prisons in the United States and have talked to thousands of inmates. This is one of the largest and oldest prison ministries in the country.

The thing I hear repeated most by well-adjusted prison inmates is, "I am glad and even thankful for being put in prison, because I would never have been brought to my senses otherwise." They hate prison, but admit that it was used by God to force them to turn away from crime and to the Lord.

Even though AIDS has spread beyond the homosexual population, we do know that in America the disease started with and has been spread by this group of people. A *Newsweek* article (March 30, 1987) said of the 32,825 cases of AIDS diagnosed in the United States so far, only 2 percent were transmitted by blood transfusions; 91 percent of the victims were high-risk intravenous drug users or homosexual or bisexual men. In addition there is a growing awareness that nobody is completely safe, as the disease could "break out" into the general population.

For those who hate God, sins of former generations can be visited on children and grandchildren (Exodus 20:5). "You mean, I must suffer for the sins of others? That doesn't seem fair," someone says. Again, God works differently. There is one certainty: When others suffer because of my sins, God's got my attention. Homosexual and heterosexual promiscuity has been slowed by fear—if not of God, then of AIDS.

A few have said aloud that AIDS is the judgment of God. That could be true—but only God knows it. We *do* know three things:

Everybody has to admit that it has focused unfavorable attention on homosexuals.

God isn't pleased with homosexuality. "And the men also turned from natural relations with women and were set ablaze (burned out, consumed) with lust for one another, men committing shameful acts with men and suffering in their own bodies and personalities the inevitable consequences and penalty of their wrong doing and going astray, which was [their] fitting retribution" (Romans 1:27 AMPLIFIED). Suffering often results from sin. It can be a direct result, as when death occurs from an overdose. More often the situation is less clear. The law of the harvest works surely in every area of life, and God has made it obvious that free sex does not please Him.

Even if, out of compassion for those who are dying of AIDS, you refuse to call it God's judgment, you are forced to say that the judgment is built into the sin, in the same way that gluttony makes one obese.

God can even use Satan as His messenger (2 Corinthians 12:7). A young woman lived in a rundown apartment. It was filthy, and you could hear a whisper in the next room. The owner of these apartments was a cheat. He hated God and didn't like his renters either. Because she was an outspoken Christian and always had a smile on her face and was always witnessing to him, he was especially tough on the woman.

One morning, through the thin walls, he overheard her praying, "O God, I don't have any food. Lord, I know You are the Great Provider. Would You give me some groceries today?"

He thought, *Well, I'm going to show that girl once and for all.* So he bought a whole carload of groceries and put them on her table. She came in late that afternoon, after looking all day for a job, and discovered the groceries. She began to praise God.

She ran to his apartment and beat on the door. She said, "I want you to know, sir, you have laughed at me, and you have laughed at my God, and you say God won't answer prayers. I promise you that no one but God and I knew that I needed groceries. I prayed this morning, and this afternoon, when I came in, my table was loaded down with everything I needed. God obviously answered my prayer."

He toyed with her for a while, then admitted, "Oh, you Christians are all alike. God didn't bring you those groceries. I heard you praying this morning. I bought those groceries to prove to you that God didn't provide."

She laughed and said, "Oh, yes, God *did* provide. He just used the devil to deliver them."

Whether you receive discipline or blessing, God is using it because He loves you: "For when he punishes you, it proves that he loves you. When he whips you it proves you are really his child . . ." (Hebrews 12:6 TLB). He says, "I am going to chastise you because I love you." Even though this isn't fun, it will be fruitful in your life.

Yes, Even When You Sin

But you've sinned and it's your own fault. You've caused your problem. Sure, you can understand God causing most things "to work together for good," but when it's your own sin, all bets are off. You are on your own. Right? No, *wrong!*

Simon Peter said, "I know how you are hurting, I know what you've done. It also happened to me. I've been there. I've cursed God, denied God, turned my back on God. I actually denied Him three times. When I heard the cock crow, it reminded me of the Lord's prophecy. I was so broken that I wept bitterly." Peter's life perfectly exemplifies how God uses the sinful things in a Christian's life to strengthen him. Even after the three-time denial, Peter came back to become the rock upon which Christ built the church.

Even the intentional, premeditated, planned sin God transforms, using it or its consequences to bring us around to His way of thinking!

Even the Little Things

God may use simple little things. A princess came out of her palace to take a bath in the Nile. Why would she decide to take a bath in a dirty river, when she had golden tubs and warm water in the palace? Maybe God helped her remember how much fun she'd had as a girl, swimming in the Nile, and she decided to try it again. As she prepared to get into the water, the princess heard a baby crying. She found him in a reed basket, floating on the water, took him to the palace, and raised him as her son—Moses. Simple things—a baby's cry saved the child who would one day save a nation!

God Makes All Work Together

In the original language, Romans 8:28 says, "And we know that God worketh all things together." It doesn't just work itself out: *God* makes it work.

But that doesn't mean all things work together for all people. The promise is only to those who "love God." If you're not a Christian, you're on your own. All the promises of God's providential care and protection do not apply. Winds of opposition will blow against you, and you'll be by yourself. If you do not already know Him, you can only claim His promises by experiencing the adversity God sends to get your attention, so that you will come to Him. When you've done that, you can claim the promises.

There's also another side of the coin of evil being turned to good. For those who do not believe, good can be turned to evil. Prayer is good and powerful in the hands of a Christian, but it can become bad: "And let his prayer be turned into a sin" (Psalms 109:7 AMPLIFIED). An unrighteous man's prayer can be sin.

Even Christ can be bad. You say, "He is good. How can He also be bad?" Christ said, "I have come to give you life and life more abundantly" (*see* John 10:10). But to many that can become a curse. Why? Because Christ is the door, and a door can do one of two things. It can be open, to let you in, or it can shut you out. However, you are the one who decides whether or not to grab the handle and swing the door wide. You decide to accept the life Christ offers, or leave it shut and reject Him. Those who do not open it will shut themselves out of the abundant life and heaven.

Christ's resurrection is good, but to many it is bad. "And shall rise again—those who have done good, to eternal life; and those who have continued in evil, to judgment" (John 5:29 TLB). Resurrection is good for those who love God. But to those who don't, resurrection is judgment. It would be better for you if Jesus had never come forth from the grave,

•

if you do not love Him. The Bible says, "Yes, each of us will give an account of himself to God" (Romans 14:12 TLB). Resurrection is good news for those who love Him, but those who have turned their backs on Him, find resurrection frightening. That's why the pagan will hold out so determinedly against the supernatural. If Christ is who He claims to be, then the unbeliever is condemned by his *own* unbelief (John 3:18).

Have you made the choice that allows God to work all for your good? If not, why not?

THE ANSWERS TO *WHYS* COME LATER

•

FIVE

•

THE ANSWERS TO *WHYS* COME LATER

I concede that if you had a series of experiences like Joseph's, you might have a hard time genuinely believing the *all* in ". . . all things work together for good . . ." (KJV). After being tossed in a pit, sold into slavery, and thrown into prison, how would you feel if you climbed partway out, and your employer's wife lied about you, accusing you of rape? Again you ended up back in the pit, down at the bottom of the prison. After all that, could you believe God was working *good* in your life?

Well, I know some people who have gone through some problems that could rival or even beat Joseph's. I've met them where we find Joseph: in prison. You may think Joseph was there unjustly, and I would reply, "So are some inmates today." But even if someone's imprisoned justly, the cause of suffering isn't as important as his response to it.

Examples in Suffering

One of the best ways to understand suffering is to look at the Bible people who went through it and learn what God was doing in their lives. Once you know what He did then, you can have an idea of how the God who never changes can work in your life today.

Joseph

Early in his life it became apparent that Joseph, the first child of Jacob's favorite wife, would be his father's favorite son. As Jacob heaped favors upon the boy, his brothers began to become jealous. Then God gave Joseph two dreams that suggested the other sons of Jacob would someday bow down before him. Obviously it was foolish of Joseph to brag about it, but he did, and the brothers did not like that at all. In fact, they finally became so jealous that they sold this proud young man as a slave to some passing Midianite traders, headed for Egypt. To cover their crime, they told Jacob his favorite son had been killed.

When they reached Egypt, the traders sold Joseph to a high government official named Potiphar. Because he served his master well, Joseph became his trusted household steward. When Potiphar's wife made sexual advances, the honest young man stood clear of such sexual cheating, but his virtue fanned the woman's frustration. Finally she unjustly accused Joseph of raping her, and the slave was thrown into prison, where he stayed for two years.

Betrayed by his own brothers, sold into slavery, lied about by his boss's wife, and forgotten in jail, Joseph had every reason to feel bitter.

Suffering that glorifies God. In spite of everything he endured, Joseph remained an example of what God can do in us, if we allow Him to glorify Himself through our suffering. Though Joseph did not see the purpose in his suffering, he continued to believe in God and act in faith. In God's eyes, how you respond to pain is more important than the pain itself. Some people today have learned that truth.

During one Christmas season, a woman named Cindy was excited, because in addition to looking forward to the holiday, she was going to have her first child. That evening, the family planned to have their usual big Christmas celebration at her mother's home. About mid-afternoon, Cindy became uncomfortable. By 6:00 P.M. she had to go to the hospital.

There she delivered a one pound, ten ounce boy. The doctor told her and her husband, "The baby is too small to make it, but we will do all we can. Just don't get your hopes up."

A couple of hours later, the parents saw that tiny, bruised child; to them he looked beautiful. They did not know they would not see him again. At 5:00 A.M. they were told the child had died.

For weeks, even months, after the baby died, a little thing like a diaper commercial or a song on the radio would bring tears to Cindy's eyes. Yet despite the pain, both she and her husband believed God had a purpose, even though they might not understand it.

In time, Cindy and her husband recognized that some good things had happened as a result of their child's death. In their suffering, they began to draw closer to Christ. Later they realized how weak their relationship with Him had once been. "We don't understand why God allowed it to happen," Cindy said. "But we hope that through this experience we'll be able to help others." She and her husband have developed a ministry to heartbroken couples who have lost a child, because their tragedy made them realize God might allow something to happen "to them," to help them understand what He wants to do "in them."

Refusing to Compromise. Faced with the trials of Joseph, many people might have said, *Well, what difference does it make? I might as well go ahead and have some fun out of life. I've always tried to live right, and look where it's gotten me!* Or Joseph could have rationalized, *Everyone in Egypt is doing it. I need to avoid displeasing this important woman. I've never had sex, and this is my chance. I'm just a poor slave—who am I to say no to my master's wife?* But he remained true, despite the temptations.

In his life we can see some things that helped him "win when the roof caved in."

Suffering Patiently. Two years is a long time to spend in a stinking dungeon. What did Joseph think about during those days? Maybe he wondered about his family and how his father responded to the loss of his favorite son. We only know that during that time Joseph kept busy the best he could. The faithful, hard-working servant in Potiphar's house was the same kind of person in prison. Often patience and endurance are required for a long time.

Making the Best of It. Instead of complaining about the food, loss of freedom, darkness, and stink of the dungeon, Joseph made the best of it. Not only did he do what he had to, he did a superior job, with a great attitude. He was like a light in a very dark hole. As a result he received even greater responsibilities: The jailer put him in charge of all the inmates (Genesis 39:21, 22).

Ministering to Others. Rather than being preoccupied with himself and the unfair treatment he'd received, Joseph was sensitive to the needs of others. Often suffering people become obsessed with their own problems, but not Joseph. When he saw other prisoners were sad, he wanted to know why and what he could do to help (Genesis 40:6–8).

Eventually the faithful Joseph became the second most powerful man in Egypt. After he helped pharaoh and was placed in the position of prime minister, God began to show Joseph some of the reasons behind the suffering.

Forgiveness that glorifies God. When famine came to Canaan, Jacob sent his sons to Egypt to buy grain. As prime minister, Joseph could arrange for his family to move into the grassy lands of Egypt, where they could graze their cattle, sheep, and goats—and he did just that. Though he had every reason to be angry with the men who had sold him into slavery, Joseph did not try to get back at his brothers. Perhaps the truth about his suffering had begun to dawn on this powerful man. From his difficulty had come the salvation of his family and the entire nation.

When the brothers discovered who Joseph was, they feared for their lives, because they expected he would take revenge on them (Genesis 45:5–8). When Jacob died in Egypt, they again thought their brother would turn mean and have them executed. Joseph reassured them, saying, "Don't be afraid of me. . . . As far as I am concerned, God turned into good what you meant for evil . . ." (Genesis 50:19, 20 TLB).

We see the same understanding of God's turning evil into

good in the life of Christ. Instead of calling down twelve legions (60,000) of angels to destroy all who wanted Him dead, Jesus chose to suffer the cross. What Satan and the Jewish leaders intended for evil, God used to achieve the pinnacle of good.

The first century, dominated by the cruel Romans, thought of the cross as a symbol of cursing. But Christ changed it forever into a symbol of blessing and redemption, and today we place it atop our churches as a reminder that suffering can be changed into salvation.

Elijah

Another example of victory over suffering can be seen in the life of the prophet Elijah. In one of the greatest victories described in the Old Testament, Elijah stood on Mount Carmel and challenged the prophets of Baal to a contest of fire. God vindicated His prophet, turning the people again to Him.

Before that day, however, Elijah experienced much suffering, as part of his training. Because God hates pride, He has to humble the believer before He can lift him up.

After Elijah had prophesied to King Ahab that Israel would receive no rain, except at his command, God told the prophet to hide by the brook of Cherith. There Elijah was fed by ravens—scavenger birds—until God sent him to a penniless widow, who would care for him. What a frustrating time this must have been for that man of action, but it was necessary spiritual preparation. Only when he had completed the course in humiliation could God use Elijah for what He had planned.

How greatly God used Elijah, when He restored the

widow's son to life (1 Kings 17:22). For the first time in history God resurrected a person, and He used a man who had had his life sustained by scavengers and a helpless widow.

Then Elijah was used in an even greater way when he publicly challenged the pagan Baal worshipers to a duel of fire. Through the prophet's faith, God demonstrated His power and exposed Baal as a phony.

Unlikely Examples

How many people would choose someone who'd spent years as a slave, then as a jailbird, as leader of a powerful country? But that's exactly the training camp God put Joseph through to prepare him for his Super Bowl of being prime minister of Egypt.

Who'd choose a man who had to run away from kings and spend his time being fed by scavenger birds to lead a nation spiritually? Yet that's what God did in the case of Elijah.

Both Elijah and Joseph are in a sense like Christ, of whom the writer of Hebrews says, "And even though Jesus was God's Son, he had to learn from experience what it was like to obey, when obeying meant suffering" (Hebrews 5:8 TLB). However, we can see the most direct parallel between Joseph and Jesus. Both were:

Sent on a mission to find their brothers—Joseph to the other sons of Jacob, and Jesus to the lost of the world.

Hated by their brothers, without cause.

Plotted against, stripped of their robes, sold for the price of a slave, bound, rejected, and falsely accused.

Highly exalted. When Joseph rode through the streets of Egypt, the people were commanded, "Kneel down" (Genesis 41:43 TLB). In speaking of the exalted Christ, Paul proclaimed, "Every knee should bow . . ." (Philippians 2:10 KJV).

From these men's lives we can see that victory never comes without suffering. But as Peter wrote: "After you have suffered a little while, our God, who is full of kindness through Christ, will give you his eternal glory. He personally will come and pick you up, and set you firmly in place, and make you stronger than ever" (1 Peter 5:10 TLB). It's difficult to believe any Christian could think that suffering is all of Satan.

What Can We Learn?

Why does God give us all this information in the Bible? Paul hands us a key when he says, "All these things happened . . . to warn us against doing the same things; they were written down so that we could read about them and learn . . ." (1 Corinthians 10:11 TLB). He says we learn from them, but *what* do we learn?

Understanding Why

To comprehend all the trials God sent into his life, Joseph would have had to have a direct revelation from Him. Sure, God *could* have told Joseph all about it ahead of time, but then Joseph would never have grown through his trials, because they wouldn't have been trials. *How could Joseph remain faithful through all that?* you may wonder. Because he knew God was good and in control of both the entire universe and the intimate details of his own life.

Don't demand an immediate answer to your suffering. Often it cannot be fully understood until later. Don't grope in darkness, trying to explain some tragedy in your life, because a struggle that brings no answer just increases your frustration. Be patient, and God will show you. The Bible gives us no record that Job or Joseph ever got answers from God during their sufferings, but later He clearly revealed the *whys*.

After the funeral of their only child—a teenage son— brokenhearted parents concluded, "Well, at least now we know why God allowed Bobby to be killed on his bike. Three of his buddies received Christ during the funeral service." Maybe this wasn't the only reason, but at least they saw one good result.

Wracking your brains to justify every tragedy is unrealistic, in terms of what you already know about God. Perhaps you will not have instant answers, and you'll have to wait for heaven to know why. But if you are patient, you *may* begin to know in this life.

While you wait, focus on the fact that you know God never makes a mistake. He has a specific purpose for suffering, which will someday come to light. Sometimes you can see part of the reason, but there is much evidence that even Jesus didn't know in advance why He suffered. Before He faced the cross, He asked the Father, ". . . Let this cup be taken away from me. But I want your will, not mine" (Matthew 26:39 TLB). In other words, if it could be God's will, He wanted out of going to the cross. But He also said

He wanted God's will, not His own. So, at this point Christ wasn't sure about the Father's will.

Someday all the reasons behind the ordeals will be clear. Until then we conclude with Paul that all things, even the death of a loved one, work together for God's glory and for ultimate good.

Looking for the Coming Victory

Paul wrote, ". . . The sufferings of this present time are not worthy to be compared with the glory that is to be revealed to us" (Romans 8:18 NAS). Just as it is possible to take a valueless lump of black coal and transform it into a priceless, glittering diamond, God changes our sufferings into something wonderful. Imagine how that lump of coal might think, if it had a brain. Knowing the facts, do you think it would subject itself to the pain necessary to be changed from a worthless lump of coal to a diamond? Obviously, it would. It would consider the fiery heat, awful pressure, and great time as nothing compared to the diamond nature that awaited it.

So it should be with us. Jesus compared suffering and the pain of childbirth: ". . . You will be sorrowful, but your sorrow will be turned into joy. A woman, when she gives birth to a child has grief . . . , because her time has come. But when she is delivered of the child, she no longer remembers the pain . . . , because she is so glad that a . . . human being has been born into the world" (John 16:20, 21 AMPLIFIED). The spiritual prize God offers can help us endure present pain.

John Chrysostom probably understood this principle as well as anyone. In the fifth century A.D. this great preacher offended the Byzantine empress with his condemnation of sin. Facing the loss of his position as archbishop of Constantinople and banishment for his faith, he countered his accuser, "Thou canst not banish me, for this world is my father's house."

"But I will slay thee."

"No, thou canst not," he explained. "For my life is hid with Christ in God."

"I will take away thy treasures."

"No, but thou canst not, for my treasure is in heaven, and my heart is there."

"I will drive thee away from man, and thou shalt have no friend left."

"Nay, but thou hast not but a friend in heaven, for thou canst not separate me and defile me, for there is nothing thou canst do to hurt me."

Many believers have had victory in hardship because they believed God was working their circumstances for ultimate good. Of Abraham, the Bible says, "Abraham trusted God, and when God told him to leave home and go far away to another land . . . Abraham obeyed" (Hebrews 11:8 TLB). When Abraham heard God's call, he obeyed and went, not even knowing where he was going.

When he at last faced his brothers, Joseph told them, "God sent me ahead of you to preserve life" (*see* Genesis 45:5). Apparently he had come to understand that God had meant to accomplish greater good through his brothers' evil.

Thanking God

Once we can thank God for what He has accomplished through our suffering, we know we have come full circle.

Joseph had done just that when he told his brothers it was the only way he could have saved them from death.

Even when we are in the eye of the hurricane, though the storm seems to destroy our lives for no reason, God wants us to thank Him for the difficult time. As the psalmist wrote, "Why then be downcast? Why be discouraged and sad? Hope in God! I shall yet praise him again . . . for his help" (Psalms 42:5 TLB).

"You *really* expect us to thank God for these terrible things?" you may ask. Yes, because even in the midst of trouble we are to praise and thank Him for trusting us with the sufferings and for allowing us to go through them. One good rule to observe is "Don't worry about anything; instead, pray about everything; tell God your needs and don't forget to thank him for his answers" (Philippians 4:6 TLB). God may choose to get us out of suffering, or He may let us endure it, but we should be thankful, knowing that either way, we can be triumphant.

Most of us find this very difficult, but *praise works.* Please wait before you decide it's not for you. Later, we'll discuss it more, and you can decide then if you'd like to try it.

SIX

WHEN GOD DOESN'T MAKE SENSE

A number of years ago, a young man named Glen Chambers was going as a missionary to South America. Excited about his new mission, he was about ready to board a DC-4 in New York City when he decided to write his mother a note, but he had no stationery. He looked down on the floor and there was a piece of paper—part of a newspaper advertisement. It had the word *why?* in big red letters emblazoned across the center of the page. He took a pen and wrote a letter to his mother around that word. He tucked it into an envelope and mailed it just before stepping on the plane.

Twenty-four hours later Glen Chambers went down with that DC-4, as it crashed into the side of a mountain. A day or so after the announcement of his death, his mother received his letter!

She couldn't believe her eyes—she thought he was dead, yet she recognized the handwriting. Feverishly, she ripped open the envelope! All she saw through her tear-filled eyes were those three big letters in the center of the page—*why?*

That's the question we always ask, too. *Why me? Why this? Why now?* But we aren't the only ones who have ever wondered.

The *Whys* of Habakkuk

The prophet Habakkuk asked the same questions many years ago. "Why? Why? Why?" he yelled at God. This man lived in about 600 B.C., when the nation of Judah was rapidly declining. Injustice and immorality surrounded him—it was something like our world today. Because God had not punished people for doing wrong things and because he saw his whole world caving in, Habakkuk was mad at God.

When you read about the terrible things happening today to innocent people, you may throw up your hands and cry, "Why isn't God doing something?" That's the way Habakkuk felt as he watched his own nation declining internally and enemy troops massing to destroy it from the outside. The Chaldean empire of Babylon was getting strong and spoiling for a war. *Habakkuk* means "to embrace" or "to wrestle," and this prophet did just that with the problems of his day and with God.

G. Campbell Morgan asked, "Why are Christians always the men who have to confront problems?" I'd answer, because nonbelievers don't have to worry about them. If there is no God, you can't blame trouble on Him, so why worry? War is war, and crime is crime. But those who believe have to ask: *How can a God of love permit this? How can a God of justice and holiness not judge those who do such evil things?*

Explaining evil, when you believe in a loving God, is the major message of this minor prophet.

Habakkuk Questions God

The prophet begins by wondering and worrying. "How long, O Lord, will I call for help, And Thou wilt not hear?" he asks. "I cry out to Thee, 'Violence!' Yet Thou dost not save. Why dost Thou make me see iniquity, And cause me to look on wickedness? Yes, destruction and violence are before me; Strife exists and contention arises. Therefore, the law is ignored And justice is never upheld. For the wicked surround the righteous; Therefore, justice comes out perverted" (Habakkuk 1:2–4 NAS).

As Paul warned in 1 Thessalonians 3:3, Satan was using affliction to destroy the prophet's faith. He began to ask, *Does God care about me anymore? Is He the one who promised to help me? How can He be good and permit this to happen? Why doesn't He answer my prayers? Is He deaf?* As questioning intensified into doubt, Habakkuk wondered, *Maybe I believed wrongly all my life.* It was time to start rethinking his bottom-line convictions.

To the prophet, God seemed indifferent. He asked God how long he'd have to call before He would hear. Having faith was easy in the sunlight, but it was tough in the dark.

Suppose you have money problems and wonder where God is. You look around and see unbelieving neighbors whose every touch seems to turn things to gold. They have no problems, compared to yours. As you try to serve God, things don't get any better—in fact, they get worse. Will your faith see you through?

When you're in such a situation, you're in Habakkuk's spot. He had called to God and didn't get an answer. Habakkuk decided God was both indifferent and inactive.

Maybe, like Habakkuk, you have called and not gotten an answer. You aren't the Lone Ranger; every Christian has this problem. Nothing seems to work, and seemingly God has let you down.

In Habakkuk 1:5–11 God answered the prophet, saying He *was* in fact doing something. But once God revealed His plan, Habakkuk couldn't believe it. He didn't like what God was doing (vv. 12–17). How could a holy God use the wicked Chaldeans to punish the people of Israel—who admittedly weren't perfect, but were far better than those pagans.

To put it in modern-day terms, though we have problems in America, we still think it's the best place in the world. God wouldn't take Russia or Red China and use that country to whip us. It just wouldn't be fair! But that's exactly what He did in this situation.

I have often felt like Habakkuk and had all the same objections. "God, how long am I going to have to pray? You don't seem to care; or if You do, You don't do anything about it. Why are the righteous suffering while the ungodly prosper? God, You are inconsistent."

What's the answer to all these questions? Some say, "Well, I just don't believe in God anymore." But that presents a problem for those of us who already know He *is* real. On many occasions He has come barging into my life, and it was clearly and unavoidably God in action. So I don't have that option.

We can't deny that He exists, but we also can't deny the reality of evil. Some try to explain it away by saying, "What looks like evil is just a figment of your imagination. Evil isn't real; it's just an error in your mind." That wasn't Habakkuk's reaction. He knew evil was real because he had seen the corruption in his own people and the even-worse Chaldean enemy.

Watching and Waiting

Have you ever felt like Habakkuk? Has the world stopped and caved in on you? "I cannot believe this is happening to me," you may have said. "If I had known and been better prepared, I would have handled the situation better."

Do you know why you weren't prepared? God didn't have a chance. He knew what was going to happen and would have liked to have spoken to you and prepared you, but you didn't stop long enough to hear Him.

Faced with troubles, what did the prophet do? "I will stand upon my watch, and set me upon the tower . . ." (Habakkuk 2:1 KJV). He left his valley of wondering and went into the watchtower. "I am going to watch and see what God will say to me," he decided.

Watching and waiting for God, through a daily Bible study and prayer, is important, but it's even more important to include time to hear from the Lord. When Habakkuk began to complain about God's arrangements, he also took time to stop and listen to Him, rather than working it out on his own.

In verse 2 God says to Habakkuk ". . . Write the vision, and make it plain upon tables . . ." (KJV). When God gave him some answers, He also expected Habakkuk to write them down. Learn to take notes when God speaks to you. As you study your Bible, ask, "What does it say to me?" Then write down the impressions God gives you.

God is saying to His prophet, "What I tell you, write down. I am not going to fail you. My word will not fail you. Though it tarries, wait for it, for it will certainly come and not fail" (*see* v. 3). In other words, you can count on God. He is trustworthy, and when He promises something, He will deliver.

You may say, "I need it yesterday," or, "By the way, Lord, if You don't give it to me by 6:00 P.M. today, I am sunk. The bank will not understand Your calendar." But what did He say? "Watch, write, and wait." Once Habakkuk stopped whining and bellyaching and started listening, God revealed the answers to all his questions.

He said five amazing things:

> . . . Woe to him that increaseth that which is not his! how long? and to him that ladeth himself with thick clay!
>
> Habakkuk 2:6 KJV

> Woe to him that coveteth an evil covetousness to his house, that he may set his nest on high, that he may be delivered from the power of evil!
>
> Habakkuk 2:9 KJV

> Woe to him that buildeth a town with blood, and stablisheth a city by iniquity!
>
> Habakkuk 2:12 KJV

Woe unto him that giveth his neighbour drink, that puttest thy bottle to him, and makest him drunken also, that thou mayest look on their nakedness!

Habakkuk 2:15 KJV

Woe unto him that saith to the wood, Awake; to the dumb stone, Arise, it shall teach! Behold, it is laid over with gold and silver, and there is no breath at all in the midst of it.

Habakkuk 2:19 KJV

Against this background of despair, God also gave Habakkuk three marvelous assurances:

Behold, his soul which is lifted up is not upright in him: but the just shall live by his faith.

Habakkuk 2:4 KJV

For the earth shall be filled with the knowledge of the glory of the Lord, as the waters cover the sea.

Habakkuk 2:14 KJV

But the Lord is in his holy temple: let all the earth keep silence before him.

Habakkuk 2:20 KJV

God assures the prophet that He loves us and is working everything out. In the second assurance, He says, "As you look down from your watchtower, all you see is the evil; but I am going to put an end to it at the right time, and the earth will be filled with the knowledge of My glory, just as the waters cover the sea. I'm going to have the last say. I'm giving My enemies enough rope to hang themselves."

Verse 20 tells us that God reminded Habakkuk, "I am on the throne, and everything is in My control. Don't worry and fret. My cause will be vindicated. Just be patient. My power and presence will be so great that no one will dare open his mouth—they'll all be thunderstruck. You have inadequate perspective and knowledge. Like a spoiled brat, you want what you want when you want it. I'm not indifferent or inactive."

Because of the thin air, your car doesn't drive as well in the mountains as it does below. A plane can't fly unless everything is right. Scientists won't send up a rocket unless conditions are just perfect. But you can have a faith that works in all situations. If you don't, you don't have the faith of Habakkuk.

Habakkuk believed what God said and in the end had a faith that worked in all situations, one that made the most of the first promise, ". . . The just shall live by his faith."

Like Habakkuk, you've probably begun to doubt God during a crisis. Maybe you've been like the disciples, when Jesus commanded them to feed 5,000 hungry people. No doubt each thought, *Should I look for another Lord? Should I just give up? Will my faith work this time?*

When you come to that point, remember God has destined you for such things. ". . . You know that such troubles are a part of God's plan for us Christians" (1 Thessalonians 3:3 TLB). In His sovereign plan, He realized pain had to be part of our training program. Though we may not agree with God's methods, knowing He is behind them is a great comfort.

"Even while we were still with you we warned you ahead of time that suffering would soon come—and it did" (1 Thessalonians 3:4 TLB). My pastor makes use of that verse in his premarital counseling session, when he says, "In the first session, I always warn every couple that I'm about to marry, 'When you begin to live together, roll up your sleeves, tighten your belt, because it is tough. So *when*, not *if*, you go through difficulties in your marriage, you have been fore-warned.'" By forewarning them, he forearms them to handle the pressures.

It is the same thing in the Christian life. You have no reason to feel shocked because you were never warned, unless the person who led you to Christ and discipled you said, "Trust Christ, and all your problems will be solved." If others have faithfully and realistically trained you, you are equipped to handle this part of God's program. Stand firm through your journey along the avenue of affliction. Only this path will lead you to victory.

Victory

Habakkuk 3 shows us a man transformed by faith. The prophet has already moved from griping and complaining to watching and waiting. Now he moves beyond, in faith.

"Revive thy work in the midst of the years . . . ," he prays in verse 2 (KJV). "Lord," he's saying, "keep Your work going.

I believe You are working. Keep on going, fulfill Your promise, and 'in wrath remember mercy.' "

In response, God gives Habakkuk a glorious vision of Himself as the Saviour of His people. "When I heard, my belly trembled; my lips quivered at the voice: rottenness entered into my bones, and I trembled in myself . . . ," the prophet reports. Like Joseph and Elijah, he had lost his pride in humility. But in the same verse, he also says, ". . . that I might rest in the day of trouble . . ." (3:16). Wouldn't you like to get to a place where you can rest in the middle of a storm? You can, if, like the prophet, you are willing to move from worrying, watching, and wondering, into worship.

Habakkuk had realized that God, in His time, at His pace, had kept His promises. He saved Israel and gave victory. Now the prophet understood that his earlier anger had come from a desire to have God do things his way.

"Although the fig trees shall not blossom, there will be no fruit on the vines, though the yield of olives shall fail and the fields produce no food. Though the flocks should be cut off from the fold and there be no cattle in the stalls" (see 3:17)—that's failure. God hadn't produced, and circumstances hadn't changed, but the prophet had! He acknowledges God's wisdom in the coming invasion of Judah—even though it terrifies him. Because he trusts the Lord, God's track record gives the prophet confidence, when he might otherwise despair. "Yet I will rejoice in the Lord. I will rejoice in the God of my salvation," he proclaims in verse 18.

The book of Habakkuk ends with the prophet's final victory, in which he thanks God and tells everyone of the strength God has given him. "He will make me to walk upon my high places . . . ," Habakkuk declares (v.19 KJV). Though he started in the valley, the prophet has moved to the mountaintop of victory.

Choosing Victory

Though God knows when the sparrow falls, it still does. Though He gives us comfort in Psalm 23, we have to go through the valley of the shadow of death. Even though God sustained Paul through the thorn in the flesh, the apostle had to bear it.

What if *your* circumstances don't change? Will you rejoice or just complain and give up?

Maybe I've read 1 Corinthians 10:13 (NAS) hundreds of times, but recently I saw something astounding in that verse. I'd never really noticed the part that says, ". . . But with the temptation will provide the way of escape. . . ." God provides an escape "that you may be able to endure it."

"What's so strange about that?" you ask. Well, if He provides you with a way of escape, why do you have to endure it?

Obviously God could choose to let you out of it or totally heal you in your situation. On the other hand, He can choose to sustain you through it and make you grow. His "escape clause" isn't an avoidance clause. He gives escape in the midst of trouble, not *from* it. After all, if you didn't have to go through pain, you probably wouldn't grow.

Habakkuk's story shows us how God uses suffering to mature us. By the end, the prophet had a powerful faith for the trials to come. He wasn't worried about the future, because he knew God was in control.

Are you living in chapter 1 of Habakkuk, griping about

God's "do nothing" administration of your world? Perhaps you are in chapter 2, not knowing what to do. You may be certain you will never get to the victory of chapter 3 until you can sing, even though circumstances haven't changed.

When you live by faith, you aren't worried. That doesn't mean you won't feel concerned about crime and injustice, but you don't lose your faith because of it. You won't become discouraged and give up. Despite your questions, believe God's purposes will be fulfilled, and you move from the valley to the mountaintop of victory!

SEVEN

GOD STILL HAS FENCES

Only Christ's life exceeds Job's as a story of suffering turned to victory, and as we look at Job's story, we have a lot of questions. After all, wasn't he faithful to God? Didn't he serve Him as well as any man? Why would God clip Job below the belt, with a real cheap shot, after he had already proved himself? It doesn't seem to make sense.

Building Fences

When he appeared before God, Satan had a different viewpoint of Job. "Have you not made a hedge around him, around his household, and around all that he has on every side? You have blessed the work of his hands, and his possessions have increased in the land," Satan accused (Job 1:10 NKJV). In short, he said, "God, you built a fence around him."

It's true! God does surround His people this way. Job's

fence might not have been made of stone, wood, or any other visible material, but God had one around Job and all he owned.

If you are a believer, God has built a fence around you. You are important to Him. He loves you.

Proprietorship

The first thing the fence shows is proprietorship. Unless you own something, you can't enclose it. But Job had been bought by God. He was His property.

Sometimes Christians talk about having God as their copilot or partner. When they say that, it's obvious they don't understand that God doesn't need another pilot or partner. He is God. He owns us. We are not our own. Because He bought us with a price, He holds title to our lives.

On our end, this means God has built a fence around us, and the devil can't destroy it. Satan can't reach us unless God allows it.

In the beginning of the book of Job, God has a discussion with Satan. "What have you been doing?" the Lord asks Satan.

"Oh, nothing," he answers. "Just been traveling up and down the earth."

"Hey, have you ever considered my boy Job?" God says.

"Have I ever considered him? Just night and day, that's all. But I can't touch him, because You've put a fence around him! I'd really like to get to him. Then I'd show You that he's not as hot as You think he is! He doesn't really love You unconditionally," sneered the devil. "But I can't prove it, because You've put that fence around him."

Satan couldn't lay a finger on him.

Value

God kept talking to Satan about Job, because He loved him. When you love your spouse, your children, and your friends, you talk about them. Likewise God couldn't help talking about Job, because he was important to Him and one of His family.

As a believer, you aren't just a number. Just like Job, you are precious to God.

A tourist, riding through the desert from Egypt to Israel, commented to his guide, "I haven't seen a fence for miles. Do they build fences over here?" The guide replied, "What for? There's nothing worth building a fence around."

Because He loves you, God builds a fence around you. He says, "You are precious. I love you. You are valuable, and I own you, so I'm surrounding you with a fence for your protection." Even if you feel down on yourself and think you're a failure, if you're filled with anxiety and want to quit, don't! Remember the fence, and know that you count with God.

Being in prison is like entering a vast wasteland. Just about everyone there has a low opinion of himself—even those who brag a lot. Prison, the supreme put-down, says, "You aren't worthy to live with the 'good' people."

One young man told me, "My earliest memories were of my parents not wanting me. They sent me to live with my grandparents. They didn't really love me. I felt rejected. When I went out to play, the children were the same. They wouldn't let me into their games. When I was old enough to go to school, I just didn't seem to fit in. All my classmates pushed me out. My teacher didn't like me. As I got older the girls didn't like me and neither did the guys. The athletes rejected me, even the hell raisers excluded me, and everyone gave me the cold shoulder. Finally in my late teens I robbed a liquor store and was thrown into prison. There, for the first time in my life, I felt accepted, because I was in with a bunch of other rejects."

Anyone who lacks worth feels miserable and may act out those feelings with bad behavior, but the solution to that problem does not lie in more parental put-downs or criticism. A negative attitude is contagious, and fathers pass it down to sons, which causes our prisons to overflow. Even those who don't go as far as prison can catch it.

But it's not like that with God. To Him, each believer is a 10. He looks at us and sees our potential. He sees the best in us and tries to bring it out. When we err, He's anxious to forgive us and take us back.

Job's Faith and Suffering

When we read the first few verses of Job, it's not hard to believe God loved this man. After all, Job worshiped God faithfully and did everything he could to please Him. In return, God had blessed Job above all others.

What happened that made the roof cave in? Satan, jealous of the way God had favored Job, began to accuse the man of loving God only for what was in it for him. What would happen if God didn't keep fences around what Job owned and the people he loved? the devil asked. So God allowed Satan to touch those things.

When Job heard that he had lost his property and children, how did he respond? Not by assuming he had committed some special sin God wanted to punish him for or by griping and complaining. Job worshiped God! "Then Job arose and tore his robe and shaved his head, and he fell to the ground and worshiped. And he said, Naked I came from my mother's womb, And naked shall I return there. The Lord gave, and the Lord has taken away; Blessed be the name of the Lord" (Job 1:20, 21 NKJV). Though he didn't understand it, Job continued to serve God. As he did so, he began to answer Satan's questions about the quality of his faith. From his testimony, everyone knew that he would serve God even when his roof fell in, killing his children. Job knew no man-made roof could protect him the way God's fence could.

Faith That Lasts

Job didn't know about the conversation between God and Satan. He had no idea why all this had happened to him, and that had to bother him. Mavis, deeply frustrated with the struggle of our grandson's having Down's syndrome, often said, "If only I could find the answer. If I could find out why this happened, I could bear it better. If I could just know *why!*"

Job didn't know why, but he still served and worshiped God. After he lost his wealth and children, the Bible tells us, "In all this Job did not sin nor charge God with wrong" (Job 1:22 NKJV).

Most of us could have understood if Job's testing had stopped there. After all, hadn't he gone through a lot? Didn't that prove the depth of his faith? Though we'd expect God to let up on him, poor Job had to suffer much more.

First he lost his health: Satan struck Job with boils—from head to foot. It was so bad, he went to sit on an ash heap.

While he was there, Job's wife came to him and cried in frustration, "Are you still trying to be godly when God has done all this to you? Curse him and die." The afflicted man tried to reason with her, "You talk like some heathen woman. What? Shall we receive only pleasant things from the hand of God and never anything unpleasant?" (Job 2:9, 10 TLB.) Obviously the two were not on the same wavelength, and her lack of faith must have hurt the loving Job.

However, feeling alienated from his wife wasn't all Job had to suffer. Next, his friends would turn on him.

Will a believer serve God when everyone forsakes him? David needed Jonathan to keep him alive in the midst of troubles. But even as Job's wife and friends deserted him, he remained faithful. Like Daniel, standing alone in the lion's den, like Elijah, standing before the priests of Baal, like Jesus alone on the cross, Job decided to make the sacrifice and serve God.

Standing firm. As Job's friends tried to reason with him, to make him agree that his own sin had brought on this suffering, he stood firm in proclaiming the power of God and his own faithfulness.

Like many people today, the three friends had the mistaken idea that all suffering comes as punishment from God. These people doggedly hang on to the feeling that all suffering is a punishment from God. That's why Scripture gives us the strong example from the life of a virtually faultless man. Job's answer foreshadows the teaching of Jesus, when He and His disciples came upon a man who had been blind from birth. The twelve asked, "Who sinned?" and Jesus answered, "No one. This is to glorify God." Though he didn't have all the answers, Job had caught ahold of this truth: Suffering isn't always punishment for wicked deeds.

For a long time, while his friends talked, God didn't seem to vindicate Job's words. It must have been hard for him to hear his friends taking potshots at him. But eventually God would confront the tormentors: "I didn't like the way you handled that. I want you to go to Job and apologize."

The Ash Heap

God directed those friends, "You go down to the garbage dump and ask Job to pray for you."

Those men must have felt pretty small. "What! After all we've said about him? You want us to go to Job? We've tormented him." But God forced them to go.

Imagine the pain they felt as they faced their friend. With burning ears and bowed heads, they must have stammered, "Uh, Job—ah, Job—would you pray for us?"

If I'd been Job, I would have responded, "Do *what?* You have the gall to come to me after all you've said?" But Job didn't say that, because Job 42:10 (NAS) says, "And the Lord restored the fortunes of Job when he prayed for his friends. . . ."

Notice that when Job forgave his friends, after the ultimate test of endurance, God restored all.

From the ash heap, a life that had lost all prosperity and had become despairing, God raised up the faithful Job. Going from owning his own mansion and having everything he could desire, to losing all his goods, family, and friends had been shattering. What a shock it must have been when God gave him back everything—twice over!

God hadn't broken down all the fences. He still had control of Job's life. While he was on the ash heap, just before his friends even came to say, "I'm sorry," God had answered Job's questions with a vision of His own power that made the man declare, "I know that You can do all things and that no thought or purpose of Yours can be restrained or thwarted. [You said to me] Who is this that darkens and obscures counsel [by words] without knowledge? Therefore [I now see] I have [rashly] uttered what I did not understand, things too wonderful for me, which I did not know. . . . I had heard of You [only] by the hearing of the ear; but now my [spiritual] eye sees You" (Job 42:2, 3, 5 AMPLIFIED).

Often people say, "When I get to heaven and see God, I'm going to ask Him a lot of questions." But as you mature, you come to understand that Job's right. When you stand in heaven and see Him, you will not have any questions. Job said, "When I faced God, I didn't ask questions."

Our Faith and Suffering

Like Job, we face troubles. Limited by our minds, bodies, and spirits, we also see "through a glass, darkly" (1 Corinthians 13:12 KJV). In our darkest nights we have pleaded, like Christ, ". . . My God, my God, why hast thou forsaken me?" (Matthew 27:46 KJV.) Whether in marriage troubles, financial difficulties, or the face of death, people have asked:

"What made my marriage fall apart? How could God let my
   wife leave me?"
"What will happen, now that I've lost my job? How will I
   support my family?"
"Why does *my* little girl have to suffer with leukemia?"
"How could a loving God let my son OD on crack?"
"Did God forget my brother? He died of AIDS!"

When others ask such questions, it's hard to peer into
their tear-filled eyes and answer. Every day we look at the
bizarre problems that fill our sick society and wonder, *Where
have we gone wrong?*

I'd like to suggest that part of our trouble is that we have
three problems Job's critical friends had. We don't understand:

God's rights
God's reason
God's rewards

God's rights. Today in America, we hear a lot about our
own rights. But who ever talks about God's rights? Does He
even have any?

If you lose your children, you might say, "I had children,
and God took them away." Who gave them to you?

"Well, after all, I built the business," you might say after
someone else has taken it over. Who gave you the strength
and opportunity to do so? As God said to Moses, "I gave you
the power to get wealthy." He has every right, because He is
sovereign Lord.

Job realized this. When he lost everything, he declared,

". . . The Lord gave, and the Lord has taken away; Blessed be the name of the Lord" (Job 1:21 NKJV).

When that happens to us, we're more likely to gripe at God, "You took *my* child, *my* job, *my* health, *my* money." All those *my*s trip us up. We think we have a right to those things, but we don't. *God* has all the rights.

God's reason.   Whenever suffering touches us, we start to look for the reason. Be sure God always has one: Whatever touches us, if we are His children, is for our good and God's glory. For those, Jesus went to the cross.

Later we'll take a look at how God can change all our experiences from worst to best and the conditional promises that surround suffering.

God's reward.   When we serve Him with no strings attached, God has a great reward for us.

You've had some great days and some dark ones, but you can be sure you aren't alone. Even though you may feel He has, God never deserts you. When Job sat on the ash heap, scratching at his boils, he must have felt that God had left him all alone. Our Lord felt deserted when He hung on the cross. It's okay to feel that way, but if you wait, as did Job and Jesus, you'll receive a quiet assurance that God is still in control.

The Key to Understanding

When we question why God allows suffering and wonder how it could ever make sense, we often forget about or ignore the sovereignty of God. If we come right down to it, we have a hard time accepting that since He is in control, He never makes a mistake. Believing that whatever happens to us is eventually for the best takes tough faith—like Job's.

Why did Job serve God, despite all his trials? Because God was (and is) supreme. He has a right to do anything He wants, and He never makes a mistake: Job understood that. No matter how hard it got, Job knew all God did was good, even if it came disguised as problems.

At the beginning of the story, God was pleased with Job. Satan was the one who accused Job of ulterior motives: ". . . Doth Job fear God for nought?" (1:9 KJV). He really meant, "Does Job serve You because of the favors You give him?"

God's fence was no secret to Satan. He asked if God didn't build one ". . . about his house, and about all that he hath on every side . . ." (1:10 KJV). You see, nothing could touch Job without God's permission.

The sovereignty of God is around you, too. Though His permissive will allows suffering, He never intends problems to destroy you. Anything that touches your life has already been sifted through God's will. If He says no, Satan cannot get through.

Beyond Satan's attack. The devil reminded God, "You have been good to Job. You have blessed him with a beautiful family, a gorgeous wife, and You have made him the superstar of the East. With his family, fortune, and fame, why shouldn't he serve You? He's just doing it to get more out of You."

The Bible teaches that God will pour out His blessing upon us if we give (Luke 6:38). But would you still give if God didn't bless? If you come to the end of this year with 10 percent less than last year, and God hasn't blessed you financially, will you still give to His kingdom? Do you tithe so that God will multiply the 90 percent? What if it shrank?

John 6 describes how Christ performed the miracle of feeding the hungry. When the bread ran out and the miracles stopped, what happened? People began to drop out. Throngs of people followed the Lord—until the going got rough. When He said, "I really want you to take up the cross and become full-time disciples," He only had twelve men. When it came time to die, He only had one of those twelve—John. Isn't it amazing how many fair-weather friends God has?

Do we give, pray, worship, and serve so that God will pat us on the back and give us things we need?

The Faithful One

When I compare the childish trivia I complain about to the total collapse of Job's life structure and his unshaken faith in the midst of it, I feel embarrassed.

It's not as if I have any reason to doubt that God is with me, for I know He remains with me through thick and thin. Jesus promised, ". . . I am with you alway, even unto the end of the world" (Matthew 28:20 KJV). He is with me when others are for me, but even more when they are against me. When I am well or sick, in pleasure or pain, He stands by me—until the end of eternity.

Some troubles are temporary, while others seem to stay forever. But He has promised, "When you go through deep waters and great trouble, I will be with you . . ." (Isaiah 43:2 TLB). When we are sick, we can know "He nurses them when they are sick, and soothes their pains and worries" (Psalms 41:3 TLB). He doesn't promise to take it all away, but He won't forget us, either. Though illness feels unpleasant, God can make our beds soft and freshen them with His presence. He makes us comfortable and wipes away our tears.

For Christians, suffering lasts only a moment on this earth. Soon we jettison our sickly, decaying bodies and trade them in for perfect ones. The pain of today is minor compared to the total enjoyment of heaven. Trapped in this embodiment, we can still thank God for the pain that builds a faith that assures victory in Christ.

I want to copy Job. Someday, if I lose everything, I'd like to be able to say with him, ". . . The Lord gave, and the Lord hath taken away; blessed be the name of the Lord" (Job 1:21 KJV).

EIGHT

When Your Brook Has Dried Up

Spiritual life isn't all struggle by any means. As a Christian you've had those high experiences where you seem so close to the Lord.

In 2 Corinthians 12:4 Paul describes one of these when he says he was ". . . caught up into paradise, and heard unspeakable words, which it is not lawful for a man to utter" (KJV). His visit to the "third heaven" had been fabulous—in fact Paul wanted to stay and never come back to earth.

Perhaps it will surprise you to learn that Paul followed his description of that experience with one about his thorn in the flesh—that painful thing from which he asked God to deliver him. And he has a pretty amazing conclusion about the two experiences: We grow more through the thorns than "third heaven" experiences.

Chances are you don't usually think that way. *What I really need is a great experience with the Lord,* you tell yourself when you're feeling a little less than spiritually perfect. So you seek those higher, deeper, greater, exhilarating emotions. If you don't get them, you may feel like a spiritual failure. But when God gives thorns instead, He may be saying to you what He told Paul, "My grace is sufficient for you, for my power is perfected in weakness . . ." (*see* 2 Corinthians 12:9).

When God told him that, Paul responded, both to God and us, "Most gladly therefore will I rather glory in my infirmities, that the power of Christ may rest upon me" (v. 9 KJV). But the key phrase comes next: "Therefore I am well content. . . ." In the Greek, *content* is a strong word that means "at rest, at peace." Even though the circumstances may not have felt at all pleasant, joy filled Paul.

What did the apostle feel content with? "With weaknesses, with insults, with distresses, with persecutions, with difficulties, for Christ's sake; for when I am weak, then I am strong" (v. 10 NAS). Examine the lives of Paul, Job, David, and even our Lord, and you will discover they lived with many trials and tribulations. However, because they understood the necessity of their crosses and had faith that God was in control, they won the battle—their faith gave them victory.

As Thomas a Kempis wisely wrote: "It is good for us that we sometimes have some weariness and crosses, for they call us back to our own hearts—not to trust in any worldly thing . . . these things help often to humility, and defend us from vain glory—for then we the more seek God."

Maturing Faith

What kind of faith is this that has the toughness to win victories? How can we have such power in our spiritual lives?

We have to understand that there is more than one way people think of faith.

First, there is inherited faith, which means you believe because your parents taught you or because your pastor or church tells you something is so. This is not *your* faith, and it will never make you strong in adversity. The Bible says that everyone has to have his or her own faith. Each of us chooses to believe in or reject the claims of Christ.

The second type, textbook faith, comes from reading about men and women who had faith or from listening to others' testimonies. Though that may inspire you, such faith still belongs to someone else: Because you haven't experienced it, you can't lay claim to it.

The final kind, proven or tested faith, is valid, powerful, and life changing. You don't inherit it from what someone else says or does. Because your belief has gone through the fire of experience, the testing has proved its strength.

The apostle Peter described the development of such spiritual power when he prayed "that the trial of your faith, being much more precious than of gold that perisheth, though it be tried with fire, might be found unto praise . . ." (1 Peter 1:7 KJV). Why does God put us through the fire? Verse 4 of the same chapter tells us it is to obtain an inheritance that is imperishable and undefiled and will not fade away. We are stretched and battered for the proof of our faith! When God allows us to go through fire, He's stretching us. Once we've been tested, we can face any calamity, saying, "It's going to make my faith complete and mature. It will toughen me. God's making me stronger, so I will be prepared for any situation."

Mature faith can't be built on textbook or inherited faith. You *must* have your faith proven in order to grow.

Suffering Purifies Faith

We'd all like to have a number of things in life, and we may pray for many blessings that we never receive. When that happens, we need to realize that God, from His all-knowing point of view, has something else in mind.

For example, when things become too good, we may get a bit off track with God. Suppose you pray for a blessing from the Father: a sweet wife, a good husband, a healthy child, or a rewarding profession. Once God gives you these, do you make the mistake of worshiping the blessing, not the Blesser? Rather than feeling thankful to God for what He has done, you can become wrapped up in that spouse, child, or job.

According to Scripture, the Lord is a jealous God, who wants us to have a commitment to Him, not the things of this world. In essence He says, "I intended you to praise and love Me for giving you those things, but you have worshiped at their shrine, and you have forgotten Me." Trials are one way God purifies our faith to accomplish that.

What does the Bible say about facing trials? "My brethren, count it all joy when ye fall into divers temptations," advises the apostle James (1:2 KJV). *Divers* means "different kinds" in Greek, so James is telling us he doesn't mean only one type—in all sorts of troubles we can have joy. "Temptations" describes trials, testings, or tribulations.

Satan sends temptations to lead you to evil, but what of the ones God sends? Genesis 22 says that God tempted Abraham, but the Hebrew word used here means "tested." Satan tempts, but God tests.

If you give in to temptation and feel unhappy about it, don't blame God. When you lack peace, joy, and victory because sin has caused you to become spiritually cold, the devil has enticed you and made you miserable. In contrast God's testings make you mature. They develop character in your life so that He can build on a solid foundation. From such trials, you can grow in faith.

Has Your Brook Dried Up?

In order to encourage us to focus on Him, God often interrupts the flow of our lives, just as He did with Elijah.

After Elijah ran for his life, to avoid the retaliation of wicked Queen Jezebel, God miraculously provided for his needs. The Lord gave Elijah a place to hide in; He arranged for a raven to bring food to the prophet, twice daily. Since Elijah stayed right near a brook, he could drink from it whenever he felt thirsty. Even though this spot might not have been his choice for a vacation, the man of faith was cared for by God—until the day the brook dried up (1 Kings 17:7). Why would God allow the brook to run dry? Because He wanted to teach Elijah not to place too much faith in the brook or the bird. God was the provider: He used the brook and bird as delivery boys, nothing more.

Have you lost your job because your paycheck had become your brook? God has done it because He wants you to trust totally in Him. Like Elijah, you'd begun to look to something other than God for your bread, meat, and water.

This principle works in areas other than our livelihood. "Lord, have mercy on me; all day long the enemy troops press in . . . how they long to conquer me," cried the psalmist. "But when I am afraid, I will put my confidence in you. Yes, I will trust the promises of God. And since I am trusting him, what can mere man do to me?" (Psalms

119

56:1–4 TLB). David had learned that you can't put faith in people or things. He had to place it in God alone.

Suffering and Glory

Hebrews 11:33–40 (NAS) lists some of the heroes of the faith. In this Hall of Fame, the author of Hebrews recounts the high points of people such as Moses, Abraham, Joseph, and others:

> Who by faith . . . shut the mouths of lions, quenched the power of fire, escaped the edge of the sword, from weakness were made strong. . . . Women received back their dead by resurrection; and others were tortured, not accepting their release. . . . and others experienced mockings and scourgings, yes, also chains and imprisonment. They were stoned, they were sawn in two, they were tempted, they were put to death with the sword; they went about in sheepskins, in goatskins, being destitute, afflicted, ill-treated (men of whom the world was not worthy), wandering in deserts and mountains and caves and holes in the ground. And all these, having gained approval through their faith. . . .

How that passage shows the combination of glory and suffering! Look at the amazing things that happened: the mouths of lions shut, resurrection of the dead, and so on. But following that comes a long description of suffering.

"Being punished isn't enjoyable while it is happening—it hurts! But afterwards we can see the result, a quiet growth in grace and character" (Hebrews 12:11 TLB). Though they probably didn't like the idea of suffering any more than we do, these people gained approval of their faith through tribulations. Theirs was not inherited or textbook faith, but proven faith that had a life-changing impact.

They weren't the only ones. We see the same alternation of suffering with glory in the life of Paul. First, he had a Damascus Road experience of blinding light, then a wilderness time of three years in the Arabian Desert, a third-heaven visitation, and a list of persecutions that we'd expect to kill the average man.

Though Paul was not the normal man, I would warn that we can draw no comfort from somehow feeling he was in a different category and that his ideas aren't currently usable. Obviously Paul wasn't physically stronger, and I don't really believe he was on some spiritually superior level. Even though he spoke in tongues, he minimized that (1 Corinthians 14). He *did* have an important way of handling problems when they arose, as we'll see later.

Suffering and glory seem to be the way God works in the life of believers. Perhaps today the body of Christ has become so segmented because some want to emphasize only the third heavens, while others only seek the thorns. But the rhythm of suffering and spiritual experience kept surfacing in Paul's life, and they should in ours, too.

Beethoven spoke of the same principle of highs and lows when he said, "The triumphant song of life would lose its melody without its minor keys." Alfred Lord Tennyson poetically exclaimed, "The brook would lose its song if we removed the rocks."

Saying that we mustn't suffer implies that God can't or won't intervene in our lives. Both ideas are unscriptural and

•

contrary to the history of the church. We know that Christians have always suffered, and it has made them strong. Believing God can bring about victory through the problem exercises our faith.

The objective fact is that Christians *do* suffer. Though they pray for miracles in their lives, God may not remove the thorn.

Even though He may not always respond with a miracle, I believe God has intervened and does intervene miraculously in response to faith. He can and will heal a sickness or problems, but understanding what God is about requires that we hold both suffering and miracles in balance. Each can bring glory to God. Peter's shadow falling on a sick man cured him, but the apostle's death also brought God glory. Though Peter was not miraculously delivered or resurrected, he became a great witness to Christ. Tradition says he was crucified upside down, because he felt unworthy to share his Lord's death.

Keeping Things in Perspective

If you feel ready to give in to despair, redirect your thoughts. Get out and look at something big—for example, stand outside in the starry night and look at the heavens. Think about how God created the universe.

A March 13, 1987, news report read:

> Astronomers peering past clouds of gas and the glare of starlight say they have discovered the largest known galaxy, a giant spiral of stars 13 times as big as the Milky Way.
>
> Researchers say the galaxy, called Markarian 348, is

1.3 million light-years in diameter. The Milky Way, in which the Earth's solar system is located, is about 100,000 light-years in diameter.

A light-year is the distance light travels in a vacuum at 186,000 miles per second in a year's time, about 5.9 trillion miles.

While you stand there, peering out into space, try saying aloud, "Here I stand, stuck on the edge of Spaceship Earth by a peculiar force called gravity. I'm breathing a paper-thin membrane called air, without which I would die. At least 10 billion galaxies lie out there. The largest yet found, Markarian 348, is so big it makes me feel like a speck on a pea-sized planet. My problems are nothing to a God who could create such an immense universe."

Then go down to the ocean and look at its vastness. Think of a God who has it measured to the last ounce. Go up into the mountains and look at what God scooped up with His hands. You'll get an overwhelming realization that the One who made it all and who sustains the universe will sustain you.

Cut your problems down to size. In a Christian golfers' newsletter called the *Links Letter*, Gary Player says:

> Recently, I was playing with a well known pro who seemed to think he was having the worst of adversity. BITTERNESS was written all over his face.
>
> "I've got so many problems," he moaned, repeating himself.
>
> I felt bad for him. Not because of his problems, but because he had no perspective on his problems. He

was bitter about things of little importance. He'd gotten some bad breaks on the course and it appeared his check was going to be much less than he expected.

But he didn't realize how small his problems were. When you live in South Africa as I do, and travel all over our continent—when you see the hatred and war and famine that cover our globe—that's literally bringing millions to their deaths, I wonder, "How important is it to have one or two bad holes?" Go to Russia or India or North Africa and see the oppression and hunger and violence and then you realize what problems are.

Too many people live in a closed-in box. They can't see outside that box. Their problems get blown out of proportion and they get negative and bitter.

In a doctor's waiting room, a friend of mine saw a mother with her little boy, who had steel braces on both legs. Ralph told it this way:

He had a pair of crutches under his arms. I looked at that little boy with a great deal of interest. To my amazement, he said to his mother, "Mother, I can walk." Before I knew it, he put down his crutches and with steel braces on both legs he began awkwardly walking toward his mother. Then the next thing I knew, he said, "Mother, I believe I can run."

I almost reached out and said, "No, son, you can't run," but something kept me from doing it. And the mother looked into his face and the brightness of his face was so expressive that the mother said, "Son, you can run."

The little boy took two steps as if he was running. On the third step his left foot caught behind his right foot and he was falling toward the floor and about to smash his little face when his mother reached out and caught him and hugged him. As she held him close and looked into his face, she said, "Son, that was magnificent. You just walked and you just ran. You did it."

I thought, *I'm like that little boy. Here I am so handicapped with my humanity and I've often exclaimed, "Oh, Lord, I can walk." The Lord says, "That's right." I yell, "Lord, I can run." The Lord says, "That's right. Run." When I attempt it and I'm about to fall flat on my face, the hand of Almighty God reaches down in my point of deepest despair and picks me up and says, "That was magnificent. You walked and you ran."*

God did that for Elijah. When the prophet had some great victories, immediately followed by awful despair, I'm sure God was trying to say something like: "Elijah, that's magnificent. You walked for Me, and you ran for Me. Why, Elijah, what are you doing here in defeat? Start walking and running again. Don't *dare* give up."

He's saying that to you, too.

NINE

The Better the Golfer, the Greater the Handicap

Everyone knows that in golf the better you play, the greater your handicap. But how often do we think about physical handicaps that way?

Have you ever thought that handicaps might not be that at all? The conclusion we come to about such "limitations" depends on how we look at them.

Twelve-year-old Karen Yates seems to have caught on to that truth quite well:

> I was born April 8, 1975 with Golden Hars syndrome. I had a cleft lip and palate, a missing right lung, thumb, and ear. When I was seven months old, I had my lip fixed. When I was four, I had my palate closed.
>
> When I was seven, I was cleaning out my desk at home. I came across a book called *Good News*. It was

just a little magazine, but it meant a lot to me. I started reading it, and I realized I was a sinner. I went to my parents and asked them to pray with me. They did, and I can't begin to describe the happiness and joy I had after that prayer. I knew Jesus was in my heart.

Oh, how happy I am to have Christian parents to help me grow in Christ and to teach me the way God wants me to act. I love them so much.

When I was six years old, we had found out that I had scoliosis (curvature of the spine). Dr. Lawson, my doctor, wanted to wait until I was thirteen to do surgery, so I started wearing a scolotron. I didn't like it, but I prayed for God to help me every night, and He did. About two years ago we found out that the scolotron wasn't doing its job. Dr. Lawson said he would have to go ahead and do surgery. We weren't sure about the procedure. It seemed so scary.

That was a Wednesday, and that night my dad went to prayer meeting. Brother Rial preached on Psalm 23. That really comforted my dad. He shared it with us, and I was touched by it, too. We started praying about what to do.

In April, we went to Scottish Rite Hospital and saw another doctor. His name is Dr. Johnston. He had done two other Golden Hars patients before. We felt this was the answer to our prayers. God let us know it was.

Time before the surgery was difficult for me. The doctor said that the risk involved in doing the surgery was being paralyzed. I needed a tracheotomy and some dental work done before the surgery, so I had that done on July 8. They waited two weeks before doing the major back surgery.

I was afraid. I searched the Bible for verses to comfort me. "Fear thou not; for I am with thee: be not dismayed; for I am thy God: I will strengthen thee . . . yea, I will uphold thee with the right hand of my righteousness" (Isaiah 41:10 KJV). "Call upon me in the day of trouble: I will deliver thee, and thou shalt glorify me" (Psalms 50:15 KJV). A verse Brother Rial gave me to claim was, "And we know that all things work together for good to them that love God, to them who are the called according to his purpose" (Romans 8:28). I prayed, and so many other people prayed. Prayer is so powerful.

I had the surgery, and the doctors were amazed at how well I did, especially the anesthesiologists, who anticipated my having breathing problems and being on a ventilator afterwards. I breathed just fine on my own. The doctors thought I would have to keep my tracheostomy for several weeks after my surgery. It turned out I got the tracheostomy taken out four days after I had surgery.

God sure does answer prayers. He answered ours above and beyond what we asked: ". . . there hath not failed one word of all his good promise . . ." (1 Kings 8:56). I told my mother one day that the verses seemed real and alive to me. Before, I had believed the verses, but now it is different. Of course, I had some depressing times while I was in the hospital, but God helped me through them. Now I'm not trying to say that I never had any emotional times. I did. I cried during prayer. I cried myself to sleep so many times, but God helped me through it.

It hurts to be different. It hurts to be stared at or

talked about. But I know I am important to God. I accept the way I am. I try to be thankful for things I do have. If you have always had all of your body parts, you take it for granted, I know. I do, too, sometimes. But the last thing that I would want people to do is to feel sorry for me. I am very happy as the person I am. ". . . For man looketh on the outward appearance, but the Lord looketh on the heart" (1 Samuel 16:7).

The first Sunday I was back in church we sang, " 'Tis So Sweet to Trust in Jesus," and it really touched me because it's just the way I feel. Let me tell you the words:

> *'Tis so sweet to trust in Jesus,*
> *Just to take Him at His word.*
> *Just to rest upon His promise,*
> *Just to know, "Thus sayeth the Lord."*
>
> *Jesus, Jesus, how I trust Him!*
> *How I've proved Him o'er and o'er.*
> *Jesus, Jesus, precious Jesus*
> *O for grace to trust Him more.*

In *You Gotta Keep Dancin'* Tim Hansel tells of one woman's positive outlook:

Consider this late-night phone call I received. The voice on the other end inquired with great enthusiasm: "What does it mean for a horse to be handicapped!"

She hadn't identified herself, but I knew who it was. Leigh was a very special friend, and we've been through much together. She not only suffers from severe cerebral palsy, but had faced other, sometimes even more severe, difficulties—like losing her family at an age too young. Her feistiness and tenacity are not only her hallmarks, but are a contagious influence on us all.

I responded to her question, "Well, Leigh, I'm not exactly into horse racing, but as far as I understand, they usually handicap the strongest horse by adding a little extra weight. It's done in order to make the race more fair."

"Yeah, I know!"

Then she asked, "What does it mean if you handicap a golfer?"

"Well, Leigh—again, I'm not really sure. But as far as I understand the rules, they handicap the best in order to make the game more exciting. The better the golfer, the larger his handicap."

"Yeah, I know. And what does it mean when a bowler is handicapped?"

After we explored a number of sports, always reaching the same conclusion, there was a rather long pause. Then she said, with bold simplicity: *"That's it!"*

"That's what, Leigh?" I replied, not understanding.

"That's it! That is why God gave me such a big handicap . . . *because I'm so special!"*

It was one of the finest statements for tenacious dignity in spite of circumstances that I have ever heard.

Leigh is a fighter, special beyond description. And because of that, Jesus will continue to "win in the end" in her life. We need more like her.

As Winston Churchill put it: "Success is never final; Failure is never fatal; It is Courage that counts."

131

Understanding Why

No one gets away with having no troubles in life. ". . . In the world ye shall have tribulation . . ." God's Word promises (John 16:33 KJV).

Most everyone I know either just got out of a major problem, is just getting ready to go into one, or is now in one. Through problems, God forces us to grow, and it's usually tough!

But often Christians don't see things that way. Instead they have an underlying belief that you only suffer if you've done something wrong, so they ask, "Who sinned?"

Did I Do Something Wrong?

John 9 details a discussion between Jesus and the disciples. Seeing a man who had lacked sight since birth and having heard from other teachers that such trials would only be given if the man or his parents had sinned, the disciples came to the conclusion that someone had to be at fault. So they asked not, "Did anyone sin?" but, "Who sinned?" The Greek word used here indicates that they were not talking about man's sin nature—the tendency to sin that we all share. They wanted Jesus to tell them what specific sin had been committed. Like many people today, they figured suffering had to come from some specific act against God's law.

What did Jesus say to the question "Who sinned?" First, it is a stupid question, because how could this man sin, if he was born blind? Obviously a fetus can't sin. What could an unborn child do that was bad enough to cause him to be struck blind, while swimming in his prenatal sac? They were trying to force Him to blame the parents, but He chose a third alternative: "It is in order that the works of God may be displayed in him." Jesus did not answer their question. There are many mysteries He has never answered. He dealt with the immediate case, but did not answer His followers' ultimate question: *Does sin cause all such handicaps?*

Nor did Jesus answer the question when He told of Pilate's killing certain Galileans without cause. Though He asked, "Are the ones that he killed greater sinners than the ones he chose to spare?" He responded merely, "I tell you, no, but unless you repent . . ." (*see* Luke 13:3, 4). Instead of giving them an answer to the reasons for suffering, He pointed them toward the need to repent before death.

Again He said, "Do you suppose that those eighteen on whom the tower in Siloam fell and killed them, were worse culprits than all the men who lived in Jerusalem?" And He answered Himself, "I tell you, no, but unless you repent, you will all likewise perish" (*see* Luke 13:4, 5).

People today ask the disciples' questions about suffering. When they face a calamity, they wonder, *Is it something I did? Could I have committed some sin?*

Just as Jesus did not condemn the blind man or his parents, He is not necessarily condemning the person who experiences trials. Every parent who has a sick or rebellious child can take heart. Anyone who has serious troubles should know that doesn't necessarily mean he or she has committed a sin.

It was such a whimsical thing: For no apparent reason, the superstructure just collapsed. It was even more difficult to explain than the roof's falling in on Job's children. At least there we saw a sort of running battle between Job and Satan.

Though it seems unfair that those helpless young people died to prove Job's trust in God, it seems less meaningful that a tower should collapse without warning on eighteen unlucky passersby! However, we assume life is a blessing and death a curse. God may think of it differently.

In the early 1960s, Helen Rosevere, a medical missionary from Britain, was captured in a Congo uprising. She was raped, abused, and beaten. During her recovery, she said, "The Lord and I got closer than ever before in my life." Then she asked, "Can I thank God for this experience, even if He never tells me why?"

God's Answers

As long as you ask why, God will not tell you, because you are against Him. While you doubt His love, sovereignty, and grace and fail to see that He is in control, He cannot get through. However, once you begin to believe that all will turn out according to God's will, because He is actively involved, He begins to reply. We've already seen that you may find:

1. Suffering is the only way you can grow.
2. God can speak most clearly to you when you hurt. As C. S. Lewis commented, "God whispers in our victories and shouts in our sufferings."
3. After you've gone through a problem, you can understand it and comfort others who experience the same kind of pain.
4. When you bear suffering well, your witness rings true to this pagan world.
5. Often God can only get your attention through suffering.

6. Sometimes you suffer so that you will learn to trust God, not yourself.

7. Victory over suffering exhibits God's power in your life.

How Many Friends Do You Have?

Here's a big one. Suffering can also show you who your friends really are. I'm not talking about your husband or wife, but a friend of the kind David had in Jonathan.

The Bible describes this wonderful relationship by saying that the king's son was ". . . one in spirit with David, and he loved him as himself" (1 Samuel 18:1 NIV).

Though Jonathan was in line for the throne, when King Saul began to attack David, he chose to side with his friend, instead of his father. Common sense would have told Jonathan that the crown would be his, if he allowed King Saul to kill David. But he chose David's love over power.

"A friend steps in when the world steps out." He knows all your failures and still loves you. Do you have any friends like that? Will anyone stick with you when everyone else seems to be against you, when you're crying out in pain, when you've fallen and can't get up? Can you depend on a friend to give you a hand and love and accept you just as you are?

Before you regret not having many earthly friends who fit this description, ask yourself: *To whom am I a friend—a real friend—regardless of circumstances?*

According to Proverbs 17:17 (NIV), "A friend loves at all times, and a brother is born for adversity." The Prodigal Son hit bottom and discovered who his real friends were. He took his father's money, left, and wasted everything he had in hell raising. Once the Prodigal found himself in a hog pen, all the people who once had been his ol' buddies took off. Scripture says he had needs, and no one gave him anything.

When a person fails, stumbles, and falls apart, everyone takes off. It always happens. Look at our Lord: ". . . Then all the disciples forsook Him and fled" (Matthew 26:56 NKJV). Only real friends will stay with you.

We find a description of the kind of love involved in real friendship in 1 Corinthians 13:4 (NIV): "Love is patient. . . ." A true friend is like that. He is also kind and not jealous; he doesn't brag and is not arrogant. He doesn't always try to impress you and never acts unbecomingly. He doesn't embarrass you or seek his own. Instead he is truly interested in you. In fact, he will fulfill these and the rest of the attributes of the 1 Corinthians 13 passage.

It doesn't matter how much hell comes against you, a friend will be there, crying, hurting, suffering with you. He will suffer vicariously as you experience pain. When you can't go any farther and just can't seem to make it, he will take your place.

Our Friend Jesus endured that kind of suffering on the cross. He never sinned, and we were the sinners. We could not hack it, and He said, "I will die a vicarious death." He took our place.

Often I think I'm too busy to be a friend, and obviously, I'm not advocating that you try to be everyone's true friend. But we all need to spend time developing a few friendships!

One young man lost his family: They kicked him out. He lost his marriage and his job. But a genuine friend stuck with him. Puzzled, the befriended man said, "I never knew anyone could care the way my buddy cared. I am nothing. I can't give back to him. I'm a failure." Then he began to recite all he had done wrong. Crying, he exclaimed, "I don't deserve to be loved! How can this man love me?"

I replied, "If I told you your friend's whole story, you wouldn't believe what he has gone through." Then I listed about five things the comforter had experienced and continued to endure as he helped that fallen comrade.

The young man before me responded, "You mean he has gone through *that*? I ought to be helping *him!*"

"Oh, no. Through his troubles he has learned that God is providing friendship, and he is also learning to become a good friend."

If you have a friend who has failed and is hurting, don't put him down. Criticism will be disloyalty. Instead, follow Jonathan's lead and say, "I'm going to love him, no matter what."

Even though King Saul accused David of treason and David was a fugitive, hiding in caves and living in the wilderness, Jonathan warned him of the plans of the king and even promised to give up the throne to his friend (1 Samuel 23:17).

By the time David became king, Jonathan was dead, but not forgotten. "See if he has any children who are alive," the new ruler proclaimed. "If you find any, bring them to the palace, and they shall become part of the family" (*see* 2 Samuel 9). David's love for Jonathan was stronger than death.

Friendships may develop because of shared suffering. War veterans will tell you that camaraderie can develop when people go through pain together. Without it, they could never have experienced such closeness. Likewise in times of tragedy and natural catastrophe, people develop an unusual depth of love and sharing. Painful times may yield the best friendships.

Freedom in Limitations

Things happen *to* me so that what happens *in* me will make me the kind of person *through* whom God can effectively work. By experiencing all this I mature to the point of usefulness. What has happened in me has made me strong.

Handicaps, whether mental, physical, emotional, or otherwise, are not necessarily negative. In fact I'm beginning to believe they can give definition, clarity, and freedom to life. God calls us to freedom *in* limitations, not *from* them.

Unrestricted water is a swamp, and because it lacks restriction, a swamp lacks depth. To make it useful, man has to channel the water into a canal. Once he has done that, he can use it for transportation, irrigation, and other practical purposes. Our lives are the same way: If we don't have some guidelines, life becomes meaningless.

On the surface we may think God made a mistake when He created meandering rivers. But when we consider the entire environment, we discover that the shortest distance between two points isn't necessarily a straight line.

God's purpose is seldom served by straight lines. Yes, sometimes He does intervene in a straight-line miracle: The walled-up water and dry ground across the Red Sea must have formed a long, narrow straight tunnel all the way to the other shore. More often, though, God allows us to wander in circles in the desert, to mature us. What we see as a circle may be His mysterious way of making all happen for our good.

Whatever method He uses in our lives, God is making us whole and complete in Him. What a wonderful prospect!

PART III

Response

When we face problems, we can deal with them in a couple of ways.

As tremendous turmoil disrupts your life, you may not like it and may feel tempted to accept one modern theology, which proclaims, "Believe right and think right, and you'll never have any problems."

Pain is something you don't want to face, but you may as well, because it will happen to you, whether or not you ask for it. You live in a world cursed by sin, and as a result problems are a part of life. It simply isn't true—or biblical—that you can somehow get enough faith to have an easy life. The people who teach this may be popular, but they haven't come up with a practical solution.

Perhaps you have sung the song "Have Thine Own

Way" during a church service or Bible study. But have you ever listened to the words coming out of your mouth?

Have Thine own way, Lord! Have Thine own way!
Thou art the Potter, I am the clay.

What does a potter do to clay? He mashes, twists, and breaks it apart. In order to mold and shape it, he has to be hard on his medium. When you sing that song, you're asking God to do that to you, too.

God *does* mold us. Why? Because He loves us. If we're Christians, He's going to rearrange our lives to make us more like Him. We can't have complete control of our lives and avoid all the pain that will help us grow into His plan for us.

As we face problems in our lives, we have two choices:

They can become our greatest motivators to spiritual growth.

They can become the tools of Satan to discourage us.

When trials come, it's up to you to choose which you want to happen. Either you move forward with God, in faith, or you sit around feeling sorry for yourself, becoming bitter and depressed. The first attitude helps you become more like Christ—the second leads to spiritual destruction.

142

Facing Adversity With Maturity

In America today, most people, especially non-Christians, view adversity as a setback. When it comes, they complain all over the place, letting everyone know about their gripes. Perhaps they don't realize that they are accepting an attitude that brings death—spiritual death. When you do that, you lose your joy in life.

The Christian perspective is to understand that adversity brings growth. So don't look at it with dread, but rejoicing. The trouble is that Christians often view their problems like pagans.

This outlook may have something to do with the fact that in recent years our country has had more suicides than homicides. We live in a world where the devil has his way, and we reap the consequences of our own sin. People have difficulty handling life because they've never learned God's way—using suffering as an opportunity to grow. When they wrongly respond, people repeat their mistakes until they learn God's lesson. Response is pivotal. The Bible shows us a unique way to handle the problems life gives us: Do the opposite of what comes naturally.

In the late sixties, when I played for the Cleveland Browns, I was moved from left defensive end to the right. That meant my stance was completely reversed. At left end my left foot was back, and my left hand was down. But when I moved, my right foot was back and my right hand down. For days I felt clumsy, because I had grown accustomed to the old stance. It took time for the old way to wear off and the new one to become comfortable. The only thing I can remember that was tougher was when I played baseball in high school. I was a right-hander and I tried switch hitting (swinging the bat like a left-hander, from the left side of the plate). It felt impossible, and after a few days I gave up. But there are a lot of switch hitters, and I'm certain I could have retrained myself, if I had kept trying long enough.

Just as I felt that changing position would never feel natural, the idea of winning when the roof caves in seems impossible to us. After all, we've accepted the idea that caving-in roofs set you back. Logically it doesn't seem they could ever help. But the fact of the matter is that you need to accept your falling roofs before you can have spiritual life in your troubles.

In talking about maturity, my dear friend and mentor Fred Smith told me maturity is the constant changing of discipline into reflex. He said very few saints have accomplished the Christian reflex state; most of us still live in the discipline-control routine. We know how we should react, and given time we will get on beam, but don't surprise us and expect the right reaction. Fred takes as his text, "those things I would do I do not," in such a case. When our disciplines become genuine reflexes, we are in the middle of the maturity road and trucking. When discipline has perfected its work, it turns gradually into reflex, and what was once unnatural then becomes natural.

Growing up in a fundamental church, I was taught I shouldn't dance, go to the movies, smoke, drink, or cuss. The church stressed very few things to do positively; mostly it said what *not* to do.

144

We also had a sort of unwritten understanding that if we went to church a certain number of times a week, that was a gauge of your spirituality. Some even said, "He's a three-service Christian," meaning he had to be better than someone who only made it to two services a week.

As I examine those *do*s and *don't*s, I notice only a couple are even mentioned in Scripture. On the other hand, Scripture says a great deal about not judging, yet this group had highly judgmental reflexes.

During the course of a message, our pastor admitted lying when he was awakened by a late-night phone call. The caller apologized for calling at 2:00 A.M. and asked if he had awakened the pastor. His response was, "Oh, no, I was up reading my Bible." Everyone laughed, but he went on to make a fantastic point. The text of the morning was about Ananias and Sapphira. God killed them for lying! Now if after the church service, he lit up a cigarette, people would think the pastor had gone to the dogs. But when he admitted to lying, they laughed good-naturedly. The Bible says nothing of smoking, but a great deal about lying.

In my early Christian life, I totally missed that which is so central to the Bible, "thanking God in all things" (*see* 1 Thessalonians 5:18), so it never became a reflex, because it wasn't one of the disciplines. In a church in which Scripture was so emphasized, we had totally missed the most-stressed principles and had made disciplines out of the only implied ones.

My reflexes were very strongly set along the lines of those things, but I later decided to change the disciplines. I felt uncomfortable at first, but it became easier as time went on.

We should be mature enough to admit that the only disciplines we should allow in our lives should be those Christ had in His! Since our reflexes are the fruit of our disciplines, the mature person is the one who progressively chooses the central teachings of Scripture and allows them to develop into reflexes by the power of the Holy Spirit. When less important, basically external disciplines are overemphasized, that which is central to Christ's teaching is usually missed. This results in a modern Pharisee, much like the first-century breed. He will have very little love. Christ, of course, puts love at the head of the list!

One of my most important disciplines is to edify my wife and children, rather than constantly teach them. The term *teaching* is a nice way of saying "putting them down." I have studiously disciplined myself to edify, "build up," rather than put them down. But get me in a pressure situation, and I revert back to the old "put down," a result of earlier improper discipline. Give me time, and I will see my mistake and repent. But as Fred said, "Don't surprise us and expect the right reaction." Thankfully, I can ask for forgiveness and turn to the more scriptural discipline and gradually develop the right reflexes, and therefore, maturity.

We are horrified by an increasing crime rate and could give in to our first reflex of "lock 'em up and throw away the key." I have gotten to know the criminals in prison on a regular basis for almost twenty years, and I've discovered that reflex to be wrong! The strong teaching of Christ is to not throw stones at anyone, especially those less fortunate. Indeed, He commands us to "visit those that are in prison" and "preach deliverance to the captives."

We all have troubles of some sort. According to the Bible, God only advances His saints through adversity, because problems develop what He wants in our lives. Though it doesn't feel comfortable, we need to accept difficulties as part of the human condition and to begin to see them from God's perspective.

God's Plan in Pain

When the troubles come and you make that pivotal decision to act in the unnatural way God prescribes, what do you do? Scripture gives us three critical responses that are the opposite of what most people would do under the circumstances. It says we should:

Rejoice
Thank God
Control our minds

These three are the *how* of winning when the roof caves in, and we'll consider them in this final section. I suggest that you read and reread these chapters until you feel you completely understand the ideas. But even after you do, take another step: Practice them. Knowing is not enough, if you don't put your thoughts into action.

TEN

EXPANDING
YOUR FAITH

Making the most of trials in your life is something like my view of chocolate cake. Recently I asked my wife to tell me what she put in hers. "Sugar, eggs, flour, bitter chocolate, vanilla, baking soda, and buttermilk," she replied. When I started thinking about those ingredients, I realized that individually I hate them all! But mix them together, put them in the oven, and it comes out as the chocolate cake I love.

God uses suffering the way my wife uses those ingredients. I may not enjoy the heartache, but when He blends it with the rest of my life, all things work together for good. In the middle of the hurt, it helps if I can say, "This is awful, but I believe it will, when mixed by God, be changed into good."

Rejoicing

Of the three weird responses God requires of the suffering Christian, the first, rejoicing, is the most difficult, according to our natural inclinations. Often people will say, "I'm not a deep enough Christian to rejoice in suffering. That comes with great spiritual maturity."

I don't agree. I think rejoicing comes through simple, childlike faith. As we face problems, if we are children of God, we can exercise faith and say, "I am going to rejoice—believing that though I don't genuinely feel it at this moment, I *will* feel it as time goes on." At first that joy may seem superficial, but later it becomes reality.

Start on the little things. Don't wait for a major crisis—begin today! If you are in traffic and the guy to your right cuts out in front of you, missing your bumper by a hair, rejoice! Learn on the small things, and as the big ones hit, you'll be ready for them.

Jeremiah 12:5 discusses footmen and floods. It simply states that if you have difficulty fighting against footmen, then what will you do when you go up against the horsemen? If you have difficulty crossing the Jordan, how do you hope to cross the Jordan in the flood stage? In other words, if you gripe and complain about the little things, what will you do when you come up against the big things?

I was talking to the Seattle Mariners baseball team, as well as the Texas Rangers, in their chapel service, when I asked, "If you gripe and cuss at the umpire when you strike out, what are you going to do when your little girl dies? What are you going to do when you get a career-ending injury? What are you going to do when your wife cheats on you?" The Lord is trying to teach us, through the so-called little

•

problems, how to face up to the big problems. He is toughening us for the Super Bowl.

It is important to go through the grief process when we grapple with tragedies like death. But if we have been well prepared by rejoicing for the little hurts of life, when we get up against these major setbacks, we will react with joy.

Through exercising our faith by rejoicing and knowing that He is going to cause it to work together for good, we get the victory. Again, don't wait for a major problem. Even when a small irritation attacks you, try rejoicing. Start with the little things and move on to the big ones.

"Rejoice in the Lord always; and again I will say, rejoice!" (Philippians 4:4). Now you see, Paul wrote this, not by his own hand, but through an amanuensis (secretary). Epaphroditus was his name. He actually put pen to paper to write the book of Philippians as Paul dictated it. I can imagine that Paul said, "Rejoice in all things."

Epaphroditus probably looked at him and said, "Paul, you're in jail. How can you say, 'Rejoice'?"

He said, "You heard me right. I said *rejoice*. And again, I say *rejoice*. (That's why it reads as it does, "Rejoice, and again I say rejoice.") If Paul had been a Texan, he would have raised his voice and shouted, "Write it like I tell you, partner."

"But how can you rejoice in the face of this terrible, unjust imprisonment? This isn't fair," the amanuensis protested.

"But, this is the very time that double rejoicing is necessary so that you don't allow yourself to be bullied by the situation."

What was Paul saying? He meant that circumstances don't make any difference. *Always* rejoice. Some scholars claim

Paul was masochistic. They think he meant that he rejoiced *because* he was getting clobbered. If you read all the suffering he went through, you'll certainly get the impression that some people made beating up on Paul a full-time job. But when Paul did not complain, he really said, "I count it gain to suffer for Jesus' name. I always rejoice—in every circumstance."

You Mean I Have to Rejoice in This?

As we read Paul's words about rejoicing a lot of us would like to register some complaints with God:

> "Happy people without troubles *should* rejoice, Lord.
> But unhappy people have a ton of problems. You can't really expect it of *them!*"
> "If I could change my wife, all my problems would disappear. Then I could rejoice."
> "If I could change my location, I'd be really happy. Then I'd praise God all the time."

Even with the most ideal job, a wonderful spouse, and a delightful location, you can still feel miserable. A change of circumstance won't make you happy. Recently I walked into a shop right in the middle of paradise. The clerk asked where I was from, and when I told her, she exclaimed, "I love Dallas. I really wish I were there." She had grown weary of Hawaii's beautiful scenery and warm weather. She longed for the changing seasons.

When people get depressed, it's often because they have false information; they often think the answer is to squirm out of their problems. They believe that when they eliminate insults, injury, and rejection from their lives, they'll be happy. They think life ought to be a bowl of cherries, yet they constantly find themselves in the pits. It doesn't really work that way.

Trying to avoid problems doesn't answer. Maybe you *do* have a bad job, a complaining spouse, and a horrible place to live—so what? Believe God is at work even in this stinking problem. Praise Him for your problem and rejoice in it as Paul did in his. You have the promises of Scripture behind you.

In Isaiah 43:1 (NKJV) God boldly says, ". . . Fear not, for I have redeemed you; I have called you by your name; You are Mine." Those are some good reasons not to fear, but He didn't stop there. He adds:

> When you pass *through* the waters,
>   I will be with you;
> and when you pass *through* the rivers,
>   they will not sweep over you.
> When [not if] you walk *through* the fire,
>   you will not be burned;
>   the flames will not set you ablaze. . . .
> Since you are precious and honored in my sight,
>   and because I love you. . . .
> Do not be afraid, for I am with you.

> Isaiah 43:2, 4, 5 NIV, *italics added*

Focus on that critical word *through*. God doesn't say He'll find you a way *around* your troubles. No, you must accept and go through your difficulties in order to find His joy and endurance. But He *does* promise to provide you with His presence in the midst of that going through.

Expanding Faith

Because God makes us go through the trials, instead of solving our troubles in a second, can we conclude that today He doesn't listen to or act on our requests for miracles? No, faith still sees the invisible, believes the incredible, and receives the impossible. Let's look at the spiritual dynamics at work in such situations.

Every time a problem arises, I pray for a miracle. Often God responds positively, because I have the faith without which no one can please Him. Believing God can solve my problem takes an expansion of faith. So I pray, "O God, heal me of this sickness," or, "Solve this problem," knowing He cares and is capable of it. Christ spoke of mountain-moving faith, and every Christian ought to have it.

But what if God doesn't respond that way? Not everyone receives healing. Each problem doesn't get a miraculous solution. Cases like this don't prove that God isn't working; they just require an even greater exercise of faith.

Why would God bypass the miracle? Scripture shows some evidence that when God performed miracles, people didn't grow. Manna falling from heaven and the opening of the Red Sea should have constantly reminded the Israelites of God's awesome power. But shortly after these miracles, the people strayed. Only wilderness suffering matured the Israelites to the point where God could lead them into the Holy Land.

As Mary Craig said, "The only cure for suffering is to face it head on, grasp it around the neck, and use it."

God could have removed the thorn from Paul, but through the thorn Paul grew. God could have saved the world in some simpler fashion than the misery of crucifixion. In this world of suffering, He chose to allow His own Son to suffer, and through the cross bring resurrection and life. He chooses to cause us to grow through suffering. But it takes an expansion of faith to actually look at the suffering as an opportunity of growth and to begin to rejoice in the suffering—to ask Him to not only make me content in it, but thankful for it, knowing that I'll mature spiritually and psychologically as a result.

Finding Victory

As we face trials, we can be encouraged that God has not left us helpless. He knows what we go through and has provided this verse for us:

> No temptation has overtaken you *but* such as is common to man; *but* God is faithful, who will not allow you to be tempted beyond what you are able, *but* with the temptation will also make the way of escape, that you may be able to bear it.

> *See* 1 Corinthians 10:13

Notice that the word *but* appears in the verse three times. They answer the *but*s most of us try out on God, in an attempt to avoid problems.

Our first *but* is ". . . but my trial, my trouble, is unique." We sing "Nobody Knows the Trouble I've Seen"; and God answers with His first *but*: ". . . but such as is common to man. . . ." No one gets a unique testing, because we all face the same things. Thousands of other believers have faced much more. Forget that excuse.

Or we may say, "It's just too much. I'm not strong enough. I simply can't cope." Look at the second *but:* ". . . but God is faithful, who will not allow you to be tempted beyond what you are able. . . ." No matter how many houses tumble in on us, how many jobs we lose, how tangled our finances become, no matter how bad our family lives, none of it is too big for God to take us through it successfully.

When we say, "I've lost it all—my business, my marriage, my health, my reputation. There's no way out and no light at the end of the tunnel," we can turn to the third *but.* ". . . but with the temptation will also make the way of escape, that you may be able to bear it." God will make a way of escape, even though we still have to face our problems, because Jesus has already faced every trial that will be laid before us.

We have no *but*s, no excuses, and nothing unique. No one can find a trial in which God will not remain faithful. Because He always limits the intensity of adversity to our capacity to bear it, He won't allow more than we can handle. Whatever happens, He makes us victorious.

Don't Delay

Now that you know those truths, what are you waiting for? Begin your joy today!

Many of us have excuses:

"When I get stronger, I'll be happy."

"When the kids get out of diapers, we'll be free."

"When I get a better job, I'll be a success."

"When I lose weight, I'll be handsome and happy."

"When I get my new car. . . ."

Our rationalizations could go on endlessly. For complex, maybe even justifiable reasons, we can avoid the wonderful responsibility of experiencing joy. Instead of making it some other time, why not now?

Rejoice in God. Don't predicate your life upon success and more success; find your joy in the Lord. The Bible says, "Rejoice," over five hundred times. Paul tells us, "Rejoice in the Lord." Nowhere are we told, "Rejoice in your success." Yes, it's right to be thankful for your professional victories, but make your main rejoicing in God. That way you can have joy even in the times when your profession fails.

The psalmist applied the truth of such joy to his life when he said, "I will bless the Lord at all times; His praise shall continually be in my mouth" (Psalms 34:1 NKJV).

If your spouse dies, and you see your lifelong partner in the casket, what will you do? There will be sadness, and you will weep, but shortly thereafter you need to say, "I praise God, because I know even this can work together for good." You need to put into practice "Rejoice. . . . Again I will say, Rejoice." As you feel the sadness of parting, you also know that your partner is with the Lord—in heaven. When you look to the future, you can know that this will eventually bring blessing to you and your other family members, and will work for God's glory.

Chose to rejoice. Have you rejoiced and praised God in the face of bitter experiences? If you say, "Well, not really," you haven't been believing in Him.

Rejoicing is a choice. When you feel depressed, you can decide to praise God and be lifted up, or you can grumble and complain and stay defeated. You can talk yourself into the pits or praise yourself into a Christian attitude of joy here on earth. When you say, "I can't rejoice," be more honest and say, "I *won't*," because if you would, you could, just by repeating words of rejoicing. As I said before, it's hard at first, like changing your football stance or switch hitting in baseball. But after a while it becomes more comfortable.

When you face troubles, remember that God works in totally different ways from what you expect. Though you may not recognize the how of it, because He uses methods, thoughts, and timings that you've never imagined, you can still trust His ways.

The book of Job says God will test us and try us until we "come forth as gold" (Job 23:10 KJV). Someone asked a goldsmith how long he kept gold in the fire, and he responded, "Until I can see my face in it." In this marvelous, though often painful testing, God shapes us until He sees Himself in our lives. Though long, arduous, complex, and even mysterious, the refining process is worth it.

We need not wait for the conclusion of trials to celebrate. As Abraham Lincoln said, "Faith is to believe what we do not see and the reward of this faith is to see what we believe." By faith we can genuinely celebrate the knowledge that in the end we will see God's face in us! We can, if we choose, genuinely celebrate the process.

ELEVEN

THE GOLDEN KEY: THANKING GOD

Not only does God want us to rejoice in trials, He tells us to thank Him for the problems we face.

That may be fine for the Jobs and Pauls, but surely God does not really expect a Christian like me to thank Him when life is tough! you may be thinking. *This sounds like some kind of crazy, pie-in-the-sky Christianity that would never make it in my life.* But taking this "golden key" to faith seriously can help you reach a new spiritual plateau in the midst of trouble.

Paul described the mechanics of thanks: "Be anxious for nothing, but in everything by prayer and supplication *with thanksgiving . . .*" (Philippians 4:6 NAS, *italics added*). As he shared in the *Links Letter*, doing just that changed the life of Christian golfer Gary Player. In April of 1960, Player met Billy Graham:

> He was one of my heroes, so I was thrilled when he invited me to his home. As we were chatting on lounge

chairs in his backyard patio I learned an amazing lesson.

"I'm so thankful to be here," I said, feeling exuberant about being his guest.

"It's our pleasure, Gary," he graciously replied.

"One thing that's always puzzled me," I quizzed, "is why so many people are negative about life. I feel privileged to be in America and play golf with the greatest golfers on earth."

"One reason people are negative," Billy said, "is because they do not know and obey God. Another reason is they are only thankful for the good things. We must be grateful for the difficulties we encounter too."

"The difficulties?"

"Yes, the trials and difficult experiences of life."

"That's a fantastic thought. It's never occurred to me."

"The Bible says: 'In everything give thanks for this is the will of God in Christ Jesus concerning you' (1 Thessalonians 5:18 KJV). So when we encounter a difficult thing our response should be: 'Thank you, Father,' and in our hearts believe 'THIS is the will of God for us.'"

"I've never heard of this."

It wasn't too much later before I had a major opportunity to put Billy's teaching to the test.

I was playing in the Masters Championship, and going into the thirteenth hole on the final day I was leading the tournament by three shots. Guess who was on my heels? Right, Arnold Palmer.

The thirteenth hole at Augusta is a sharp dogleg to the left. A creek zig-zags in front of the tee box all the way around the dogleg and finally swings in front of the green. It's not a long hole, but the creek comes into play on the left and in front of the green.

My drive was on the right, safe, but too far back to attempt to reach the green. I knew the safe second shot was to the right, away from the creek, but the crowd was so jammed up on that side of the fairway that it would take me ten minutes to have them all move. Impatiently, I hit my shot. I missed the crowd, but my ball bounded down the left side and plopped into the creek. Before I knew it I'd made a disastrous "seven" on a hole I should have made a four and no more than a five.

My first thought was what a stupid error I'd made! All I had to do was take some time and ask the people to move.

Then, suddenly, some thoughts went flashing through my mind. The night before, my good friend, Tom Nieporte, and I had read the chapter on "Adversity" from Thomas a Kempis: I recalled him saying something like: "It's good that we're tested . . . there can be profit from our adversity." Then Billy Graham's words came to me: "Thank God for the difficulties, Gary, not just the good things."

I felt a new charge of energy. "Thank you, Lord, for letting me make that seven," I said, "now I have an opportunity to show what I'm made of."

All during my life when I'd make a monstrous score like that, I'd feel the wind being knocked out of me. But this time something different happened. When I walked up to the fourteenth tee I really felt strong—as strong as any time during the day. I marched up the tough fourteenth hole and made a good par.

But on the fifteenth, another fairly easy par five hole, I blew a short putt and made a six. Now Arnold and I were tied and all the momentum had swung to him. Instead of thinking about how poorly I had played the fifteenth, I made myself say: "Thank you again, dear Lord. Now let's see what can happen."

I parred sixteen, seventeen and on eighteen watched Arnold blast out of the bunker across the green and end up with a double-bogey six. Fortunately, I remained steady, made par and won my first Masters.

I treasure that win, but the real victory was an inner victory. The prize I won was more important to me than the coveted green jacket I have in my bedroom closet. That prize being the lesson that has stuck with me for more than twenty years. That when I'm willing to change my mind and say: "Thank you for the difficulty, Lord," great things happen. It's the key to helping me face every adversity.

It's fantastic what blessings this country enjoys compared to any other country in the world. Everytime I set foot in this great country my heart beats with thankfulness. I don't want to be misunderstood. I'm not saying I'm always thankful and life is always shiny and rosy. I confess I'm not as thankful as I ought to be.

Right now I'm having a difficult battle against loneliness. When I travel abroad without my wife, Vivienne, and the family, as I do most of the time, I get weary and dreadfully lonely at times. And it's as hard now to say: "Thank you, Lord for this trial," as any time in my career.

Just Thank Him

Recently, in our prison ministry, we had contact with a boxing champion who had experienced a tremendous conversion while in maximum security. He began to lead a Bible study in his cell, and some other inmates began to tease him. After controlling his temper for several days the boxer finally tired of it and told them if they did it again, he would take care of them. Sure enough, the next day, the same cons began to bad-mouth him; the new Christian KO'd them in short order. When they came to, the inmates said, "We thought you were into that book that teaches you should turn the other cheek!"

He looked at them inquisitively and commented, "Oh, really? I hadn't read that far yet."

Thanking God in the midst of trials isn't something you have to have read the whole book to understand. It's not reserved for super-Christians, and there isn't a big secret about it. Just do it! If you're thinking, *I can't*, still thank Him by faith. You may not feel very thankful, but do it anyway. Faith can say, "Thank You, God," when something bad happens.

What Does Scripture Say?

We've heard some teachings on thankfulness, whether at a holiday church service or in an informal Bible-study group. Let's take a deeper look at what giving thanks means.

Simply thank Him. Some Bible teachers make a big to-do about the verse that says, "In every thing give thanks . . ." (1 Thessalonians 5:18 KJV), pointing out that the key word is *in*, not *for*. But they ignore Ephesians 5:20 (NAS), "always giving thanks for all things. . . ." Don't tie yourself up in such hair-splitting arguments. Whether you thank God *in* or *for* isn't as important as thanking Him that He will work it out.

Pray in faith. Philippians 4:6 (NAS) commands us: "Be anxious for nothing, but in everything by prayer and supplication with thanksgiving let your requests be made known to God."

Praying and giving thanks to God for a problem requires faith-strengthening discipline. Since your trial came to remind you to exercise your faith, God will turn it to good. Therefore you need to pray something like: "Thank You, God, for allowing me to lose my job, because I know You will find me a better one." If He doesn't, even that is best.

Is it God's will? When Scripture says, "in everything give thanks: for this is the will of God . . . for you" (1 Thessalonians 5:18 NKJV), it doesn't say that everything that happens to you is God's will. The problem itself may not be His will at all, even if the result in your life is.

However, just as Paul could be thankful he was put in prison to win his jailers, you can give thanks for the trial that proves your faith, because by reacting in faith and praising Him, you are pleasing God. Everything that happens to you is either the will of God or in His permissive will. Though He may not have set up the situation, God has allowed it in your life for a purpose. Thankfulness is the only right attitude, whether suffering has no apparent reason or one soon becomes clear, as when Paul won the jailer to Christ. It's not super faith you need, just the childlike faith to *do* it!

Psychological Responses

In the face of something negative, we may have over-whelming psychological reactions that hinder us from taking action that pleases God.

Fear and Anger

Our first response in almost any bad situation includes fear and anger. If you lose your child in a mammoth discount store, you begin by pleading, "Where is my child?" but once you find him, you become angry and demand "Why in the world did you run off?"

As you drive down the highway a car darts out from a side road. First you gasp in fear, then you mentally yell at the driver, *Why did you do that? You could have killed us all with your careless driving!*

Under such circumstances, natural reactions are motivated by instinct. Christian reactions to problems come from knowledge.

According to knowledge. Christian psychologist Bob George tells this story:

> I was on a plane not too long ago, and there was a guy sitting next to me who had white knuckles. He was frightened. This was his first plane trip. As we were flying along we hit an airpocket, and he grabbed his armrests and demanded, "What happened? Are we crashing?"
> I said, "No, that's just an airpocket."
> "Oh," he said. "You mean that's normal?"

"Yes, that's normal."

We started to land, and the landing gear started down, and he heard that grinding noise underneath the plane. He said, "Is the bottom of the plane falling out?"

I said, "No, that's just the landing gears going down. That's not bad, that's good. You'd better hope they go down, or we can't land."

We hit the runway with a screeching noise, and he identified that with a skidding noise before a car wreck. He questioned, "Are we crashing?"

I said, "No, that's just the wheels hitting the runway."

"Oh, I see," he said.

Then the rear thrusters came on, and he just knew we were taking off again. I said, "No, that's just the way the plane stops itself."

You see, that man reacted according to ignorance, not knowledge. Now, the next time he flies, when the plane hits an airpocket, he'll know that it's not a crash. When he hears the screeching noise, he'll know that it's not a wreck. When he hears the rear thrusters, he'll know it's just the way the plane stops. He'll react according to knowledge.

When something bad happens in their lives, most people don't react according to knowledge, but with fear and anger. Few put into practice the truth that God has planned that everything will work out for good for those who love Him. Scripture promises, "And you shall know the truth, and the truth shall make you free" (John 8:32 NAS), but many of us are so locked up in our natural reactions that we can't live that way.

168

Grief Processes

At this point someone's probably wondering, *What happens if God takes something from me? Don't I still have to go through all the psychological grief processes, when I experience a loss?* Probably so, but let's place emphasis on the word *through*. We must not linger in grief. Staying in it too long denies the very truth that sets us free.

The Bible tells of many who sought healing and had victory, but it also tells of people who got bogged down. It's up to you: You can talk yourself into a hole or praise yourself onto a mountaintop. Allowing yourself to become bitter and bellyaching against God leaves you depressed and may block Him from helping you. He can't give you His best when you wallow in unbelief. Only once you accept your problem, rejoice in it, and thank God for it can His power give you inner joy and release. "And you shall know the truth, and the truth shall make you free." The truth is that God can only work in our lives to make all work for good if we carry out the conditions. If you praise Him—whether you raise your hands and shout or quietly thank God in the depths of your soul—you can dwell on your blessings, not your problems.

Victory in Christ.   Instead of accepting God's role in painful situations, some people have accepted the lie that everything will work out by itself. They have ignored the truth of Scripture that *God* works everything to good.

The Bible is extremely clear on this point: We can "win when the roof caves in," but we can also lose, if we don't carry out the conditions. Responding to adversity improperly will destroy you, but it's never God's purpose to ruin you.

He plans to build and strengthen you. Despite the fact that the roof caved in on all Job's children and everything else in the world of importance to him, Job was victorious, because he immediately reacted in a godly way. "Though he slay me, yet will I trust in him . . ." (Job 13:15 KJV). Job never lost the complete confidence he had in God, believing He was at work.

Seeking to cope by feeling sorry for ourselves or dwelling on the bad in the situation moves us toward defeat.

In and of itself suffering is bad. Having a child born with a mongoloid condition is awful. Losing a husband or wife hurts terribly. But no matter what the problem or hurt, we know that we have One who goes through it with us.

On the cross, our Lord unjustly suffered injury, insult, and rejection. No trial of ours could compare to what happened when Jesus " . . . came unto his own, and his own received him not" (John 1:11). But Christ's accepting the suffering brought us salvation.

After Jim Elliot and four other missionaries had been killed by the Auca Indian tribe in South America, *Life* magazine concluded these men had wasted their lives. What the article did not tell was that Jim's wife and another missionary's sister went back to this tribe and began to convert them to Christ. Had the five men really wasted their lives? No, because their deaths became the means of salvation for many people.

Jim Elliot's wife simply met the condition of rejoicing and thanking God. Her powerful testimony transcended language barriers. As she followed Christ as the pattern for her life, God worked everything for good. Despite her grief, Elisabeth Elliot gave her life into the hands of the sovereign

God, to use as He saw fit. That meant going in to those Indians, and showing them His love with a thank-God attitude.

Defense Mechanisms

Another psychological response that can interfere with our spiritual walk is the defense mechanism. If you hit me in the face, the next time I see you coming, I'll protect myself. Though you get away with it the first time, when it comes to the second one, I'm prepared. I've developed a defense mechanism.

Of all the emotions, we most hate depression. Though we may pay money to be frightened by a scary movie, and we like to laugh or even cry, no one wants to feel depressed. We all have a defense mechanism against depression.

Psychologists agree that defense mechanisms for depression take many forms.

A child may use exhibitionism—yelling, screaming, and crying, without one tear—to avoid depression. Later in life it may show up in suggestive dress or loud behavior.

Others use silence as a weapon. They withdraw, saying, "I'm going off by myself. You'll never see me again." People may cling to others in defense.

Others attack, lash out, and fight back. Some punish themselves, becoming depressed and despairing. If that continues long enough, it can end in suicide.

Depression can tell us that a person has allowed emotions to control him or her. Scripture says that the Christian response to a depressing situation is different. You have to thank God for the problem, knowing it will work together for good.

You may say, "I can't do that." You can and you *must*. Do it by faith.

Faith means you believe in advance that something good will happen. Even though you can't see the good thing God is working, you believe so strongly that you thank Him ahead of time.

Seeing the Good

My pastor told me a church member came to him and said, "I've got one daughter, my only child. She's seventeen, and she ran off with a twenty-nine-year-old man. They're using drugs and alcohol. They've been gone three weeks, they're not married, and they're living together."

Brother Rial tried to encourage the father and help him, but after about an hour and a half, that man was in total despair. Finally, my pastor remembered the passage from Philippians 4 and asked, "Have you thanked God for this thing?" Then he showed the man all the passages I've already shown you.

The father replied, "Pastor, you don't understand. She's my only daughter, she's seventeen, she's run away with a twenty-nine-year-old man. They're on drugs and alcohol; I don't know where she is, and I'm worried out of my mind. What do you mean, 'thank God'?"

"You can thank God for it, knowing it will work together for God's glory and her good. Would you be willing to thank Him?"

"I don't feel thankful," the father objected.

"Would you thank God anyway, by faith?"

"Yes," the man answered, and they knelt together and thanked God for this horrible thing.

Three days later, his daughter came back. She was genuinely converted and is now in vocational Christian service. Because her father thanked God, in faith, for something that appeared evil, I believe God turned it to good.

You may protest, "I feel so hypocritical when I thank God, because I don't feel thankful." Then pray like this: "Lord, I don't feel thankful, and I don't genuinely mean it when I thank You. I'm just obeying Your Word. Because You told me to thank You, I'm doing it by faith."

Faith means believing prior to the reality that a thing that is not now true shall be. Pray like this long enough, and you will begin to mean it. Then you can genuinely pray, "Thank You, Lord, because I know it will work together for good, and I wait expectantly to see how." Soon it becomes comfortable and real.

It Does Work!

When I tell you all this, I'm not just passing along a theory. I've practiced it repeatedly as I've come to terms with the reality of my grandson Billy Ray's having Down's syndrome. I told you of Mavis's reaction to it. Here's mine:

> I have a little grandson, and he's the most fantastic little boy in the whole world. I remember the day he was born. I thought, *Man, he's going to be president, or maybe he'll be a pro football player like his father and grandfather before him.* I was going to be the perfect

grandfather. I had made some mistakes with my own kids, but I was going to do a better job this time around.

Then on the second day of his life, we discovered that he had Down's syndrome. That meant he could never play football, for he would never be physically full strength. He could never be president, because he would always be a little or even a great deal retarded. I was crushed. I felt hurt personally, but more for my grandson and his parents. Then we started to notice a peculiar thing as he began to grow. Billy Ray has an amazing amount of love. Every time he sees me, he goes nuts. He gets into my lap and hugs me and kisses me for fifteen, twenty, or even thirty minutes. If his little brothers give me fifteen seconds, I'm lucky. But Billy Ray gladly sits in my lap and hugs and loves me. I have to be careful not to favor him over his so-called normal brothers.

Recently I was at his house, and he had a little car. He was down on the floor playing with the car. In my suit and tie, I got down on the floor on my belly with him. Billy Ray said, "Ooden-ooden, ooden-ooden, ooden." I smiled at him. Immediately he repeated, "Ooden-ooden, ooden-ooden." I smiled at him again. I finally realized he wanted me to do it, too, so I joined him, "Ooden-ooden, ooden-ooden." Billy Ray answered, "Ooden-ooden, ooden-ooden." People came in and out of the room, stepping over our bodies, spread-eagle on the entrance floor. I was going, "Ooden-ooden, ooden-ooden," pushing the car in front of my face. My son said to an amused friend, "That's my dad."

174

I seldom see anyone big enough to make me get down on my belly and play "ooden-ooden" with the ease that Billy Ray can. He gets me down with one nod of his head and one motion of his hand.

No one ever stands quite so tall as when he's big enough to get down on his belly and have an "ooden-ooden" attitude with his wife and his children, his grandchildren, or his friends. We need to be able to hug them close to us, the way I did my little (twenty-four-year-old) girl the other day. I said to her, "I think you're fantastic, and I love you, and I know you're going to have an extremely fulfilling life."

I've always done that sort of thing, but Billy Ray has made it a lot more comfortable. Before it seemed unnatural, but now it seems right and good. We need to place our values not on things, but on people—starting with the Lord, then the family, and finally reaching out to the darkest corners of the world.

Don't misunderstand. I struggled at first. Like Mavis, I questioned. But I started to rejoice and thank God, even though I felt miserable. At first being thankful seemed hollow and phony. However, soon my thankfulness became real, and I even began to feel it a little. Before long, deep and genuine thankfulness came, and I felt abounding joy!

Then I noticed Mavis resented my joy. She thought I was superficial. Worse, she thought I didn't understand her hurt. Truthfully, I didn't. I tried to get her to try the "rejoice and thank God" way to victory, but she wasn't ready for it. I made the mistake of trying to push her in that direction. She rebelled, so I left her alone; that, too, was a mistake, because she felt isolated.

I failed to be the comfort I could have been to her. Obviously the only real comforter is the Holy Spirit. But I could have gently led her to turn to Him by faith. I became too pushy about this exciting principle and rejoiced in God's presence, but failed to lead Mavis in a way she was ready for.

Though I wrote this book partly to struggle with my own understanding of how to win when the roof caves in, I had another goal, too. I wanted to draw others along, without bruising them in the process. As you've read I hope that has happened in your life.

TWELVE

YOU CAN CHOOSE YOUR THOUGHTS

The third and final prescription God gives us for healing our negative responses to trials is that we control our thoughts.

"But I don't feel as if I can do that," you may reply. If so, the word *feel* shows you're right on target. Before we can control our thoughts, we have to become aware of their relationship with emotions.

Struggling for Control

Like spoiled children, emotions insist on having their own way. But give them control of your life, and they will lead you into the slough of despond and leave you there.

When you allow your mind to freewheel and do not bring it back to the faith stance, negative emotions will always dominate it. Jerk your thinking out of depression and focus on the positive possibilities. This pushes out all your destructive mental pictures of failure.

Why is this important? Your emotions are a direct result of your thoughts!

Paul's words ". . . whatever things are true. . . . whatever things are lovely, whatever things are of good report. . . . think on these things" (*see* Philippians 4:8) show us the mature Christian's response to trouble. Think on things of faith, and your emotions will follow. Choose to dwell on the great things God will do, in spite of your collapsing roof, and He will give you victory.

If you say, "I feel jealous," you actually mean you're thinking jealous thoughts. If you say, "I feel angry," you have been thinking angry thoughts. To reverse the pattern, focus on changing your thinking, not your emotions. Soon your emotions will alter.

When I face a trial, to avoid feeling depressed, I have to think about how God will turn this to good. I've got to thank God, knowing that even though this may be evil, God has promised wonderful results in my life.

If I rejoice, I cannot become depressed. While I'm thanking God, I can't give in to despair. "Fine," you say, "but that's not easy." You can do it—by faith. Even though you don't feel like it, rejoice and thank God anyway. At first you will have an ongoing struggle for control, but after the new way of thinking wears grooves into your mind, it will become an automatic thought pattern.

Overcoming the Impossible

Everyone has a price and a breaking point. Everyone can thank God up to a point.

Can I thank God for losing my job? *Yes.*
Can I thank Him if I lose my arm? *Yes.*
If I lose my wife? *Yes.*
If I lose my reputation? *Yes.*

But when you pass a certain point the rejoicing may become impossible and thanksgiving will stop.

You say, "I'm no Job. I can't say, 'Though He slay me, yet will I love Him.' I know Job, Paul, and Christ suffered more than I, but I'm not in their league. I'm just an everyday Joe [or Jane]."

But these heroes are the pattern. We win victory just as they did. Paul endured an intense suffering unimaginable to most twentieth-century Christians. He applied the principle of rejoicing out of necessity; his deep pain demanded it. One reason Paul said, "I pray without ceasing," was to fight the pain and replace Satan's attacks with joy, so his mind would not give in to depression.

In my book *Expect to Win* I tell how a similar reinforcement worked in my football career:

> I became so convinced of the power of the mind that I engaged in a project that had monumental impact on my performance in football. I made tapes of little talks to myself, about seven minutes in length, on my recorder. The cassette sounded like this:
>
> "Charge. Charge. Every time the word *charge* floats through your mind, it will activate all the suggestions on this tape. Dominate your opponent. Dominate him. Fire across the line, overpower him. Feel his body crumble beneath your power. Throw him down on the inside, rush to the outside, and sack the quarterback.

Pursue, pursue, pursue. Pursue until you hear the whistle. On running downs, destroy the blocker. Fire through the ball carrier. . . ." On and on the tape went for seven minutes, filled with powerful, positive suggestions concerning things I would accomplish during the game. I was convinced that this type of programming would promote mental pictures that would gravitate toward my playing in a super way. These suggestions would program my subconscious mind and during the game they would be "played back" when I said the word *charge* to myself. "Charge!" would be the mental electrode that would trigger the powerful suggestions in the tape. So, I listened to that tape in the mornings several times on my way to work, before going to bed, and over and over again all week long prior to the game.

But something went wrong. In the game, I played the most horrible football I've ever played in my life! In the film-study session the following Tuesday morning, the coaches were yelling and screaming at me, saying, "You hit an all-time low! You were terrible!"

After viewing the film of that particular game, I went out of the film-study session smiling. You might ask, "Why were you smiling after playing such a horrible game and getting chewed out by your coaches?" It had dawned on me in the study of the films that *I was playing precisely in the way I had put the suggestions into my subconscious.* I had said, "Charge. Charge," in a rather hypnotic tone, and the whole mood of the tape was in a monotone—almost as if I was just waltzing through my assignments . . . and gliding through my responsibilities in a sleepy manner. I knew if I could change the tone of the tapes, I would also be able to change the way I would perform in the game.

I went back to my room, and began to develop a new recording. This time the tape was literally shouting with emotion and power. "CHARGE! CHARGE! Every time the word *charge* explodes out of your mouth, it will activate all the suggestions on this tape! DOMI-NATE YOUR OPPONENT! DOMINATE HIM! . . ." It was done in explosive bursts of energy with great enthusiasm and shouting.

The next week, we played against St. Louis. All week long I listened to the tapes of shouted commands many times every day, and finally I was on my way to the game with the team. I made a deal with myself that I would listen to the tape repeatedly until we arrived in St. Louis. We flew for about an hour and a half aboard a chartered plane, and when we reached St. Louis, it was fogged in. So, we circled St. Louis for another hour and a half, and wound up flying to Chicago, where we boarded a bus and slowly journeyed all the way back to St. Louis. It took us a total of 13 hours to get there, and I listened to this tape the entire time. I rewound and played it literally hundreds of times until I feared it would collapse with fatigue, or the batteries would wear out. But I discovered a great truth. Consciously, we tire of hearing the same thing over and over again, but the subconscious never tires. Repetition simply reinforces the message.

The next day, I was literally brainwashed with the commands recorded on my tape. I overpowered my opponent and dominated him as the tape suggested. I pursued him until the whistle. I started doing things I'd never done before. I rushed the passer early in the game. Just as I was about to sack him, he released a short pass. The receiver caught the ball and ran zig-zagging for the goal line. I pursued even though I normally would have been satisfied with the pressure I applied to the quarterback, without chasing the receiver. He was delayed by eluding tacklers and I tackled him seventy yards downfield. In the film-study session, the coaches raved about my making a tackle seventy yards downfield after rushing the quarterback. It was programmed in so well that it was a reflex action. I was operating like an efficient robot performing obediently according to my programming.

Maybe that was the norm. I was simply discovering the mechanism of God's creation. He has equipped me with a guidance system called the "subconscious." This system is instructed through the picture-producing brain. These images are stored and played back on cue. What we call "luck," good or bad, is just the tape we happen to trigger in the subconscious which plays back just as it went in. The trick is to put only positive tapes into your mind. That is the only way to insure your results.

Finally, three plays before this game was over, I literally fainted in exhaustion. But I can honestly say that I've never played such fantastic football in my life. You see, my subconscious mind had pushed me to carry out the suggestions on the tape, precisely as I had imagined.

The Importance of Repetition

Because of the necessity of all-out preparation for an ultimate performance, I used intense mind control. Paul also determinedly focused only on winning thoughts when he prayed without ceasing. I can imagine that formulas like "I can do all things through Christ who strengthens me" (Philippians 4:13 NKJV) made up his prayers.

Because they are aware of the verse "do not use vain repetitions as the heathen do . . ." (Matthew 6:7 NKJV) many Protestant Christians fear any kind of repetition in prayer. But they have not considered the word *vain* in that verse. It is not vain to repeat anything that builds up your faith, as in Paul's admonition "Rejoice. . . . Again I will say, rejoice!" (Philippians 4:4 NKJV).

Early Christian martyrs practiced such repetition. *Foxe's Book of Martyrs* says, "as they were being burned alive, they were rejoicing and singing praises to God." You can't murmur against God and sing His praises at the same time. You can't "thank God in all things" while you feel sorry for yourself.

Replacing negative thoughts with positive ones is the key to such a faith-filled response. Put believing thoughts in the place of unbelieving ones that float through your mind. Picture the reality of something good happening in your life.

Am I merely recommending a psychological technique here? Could we compare it to whistling as you walk through a graveyard, to fool yourself into not feeling frightened? Or is it God's way of causing Christians to grow by exercising faith? Whether I'm recommending psychological or theological truth, truth is truth. Undeniably psychologists agree that reacting with thanksgiving is better than giving in to bitterness, depression, or anger. But the faith reaction also pleases God and brings His blessing.

When I used those mind-control techniques for playing a football game, I was getting in line with the way God created me mentally. But I also put myself in a position where God could honor my faith and empower me to play well.

Is It Christian?

In some Christian circles all mind control is criticized and called pagan. I disagree. Psychological truth and Christian truth can live together in harmony, strengthening each other. Psychology seeks to discover how God made us mentally, and a better understanding of that can only help us, as long as God is on the throne of our lives.

Obviously you need to feel concerned about who has control of your mind. Either Satan or the Holy Spirit is in charge. Check who dominates by asking if your thoughts are positive or negative—of faith or unbelief. A humorist suggested that two dogs fight for control of your life. Only one wins at any given time. Which? "The one you say 'sick 'em' to."

If you lost your job, I hope you thanked God, knowing He would work it for good. If you gave into defense mechanisms, you'd only become more depressed. You lost your job, so you became bitter and withdrew. When you went to look for another one, your depressed attitude showed. Most likely you mumbled what you're thinking: "You don't want to hire me, do you?" Obviously you *weren't* likely to be hired.

But if you say, "I rejoice and thank God for losing my job, because this will work for good. I can't wait to see what wonderful new job God has for me," you won't become depressed. Because you'll feel victorious, you are more likely to get a better job. God's is the best way, and the alternative is so poor.

Pity parties, dwelling on the horrible ramifications of bad situations, "poor me" thoughts, or anything other than rejoicing in God's working in the situation is unbelief. Check yourself. If you allow your mind to dwell on or entertain losing scenarios, you take the first step toward full-scale depression.

At the age of forty-five, William Johnson worked in a sawmill. In the middle of the Great Depression, he was fired and went home to tell his wife and children he had lost his job and had nowhere else to turn. He got on his knees and said, "God, I am going to depend on You for a new job." In response, God impressed him with this thought, *I have been trying to get your attention. I want you to mortgage your home and go into the building business.*

Johnson argued, "But Lord, in the Depression? This is laughable."

God seemed to say, *Do you want a way out? Do you want prosperity? Do as I say and obey Me.*

So Johnson mortgaged his home and went into the building business. In five years he had become a multimillionaire. Today he says, "I wish I could find that man who fired me. I want to thank him. It took that for me to find God's will for my life."

Every time I pass a Holiday Inn I'm reminded of William Wallace Johnson, who had to go through hardship so God could get his attention and he could build a great motel chain.

Trying to avoid troubles is unrealistic. Everyone gets his or her share. As someone said:

Troubles

I've got them
You've got them
Adam had 'em.

They can be stepping-stones or walls in your life. It's up to you. Make them stepping-stones.

THIRTEEN

CONSTANT WINNING!

In a first-century victory parade, a Roman general rode into Rome, standing proudly in his chariot. Behind him came captured enemies, chained to more chariots. As they looked at the practically naked captives, the crowd would laugh and say, "Is that the enemy? Is that the most feared nation?" Stripped of their armor, weapons, medals, and any trappings of power, the opposing soldiers became harmless.

When we stand in the Judgment and see Satan and all his demons cast into the lake of fire, we will respond much the way the Romans did to those conquered men. Some of us will say, "Is that what we were so worried about? Were we so afraid of *them*? Why, we have nothing to fear from Satan and his demons—they are conquered enemies." We'll see the truth of Paul's words in Colossians 2:15 (NAS) "When He had disarmed the rulers and authorities, He made a public display of them, having triumphed over them through Him." Like the Roman generals of that century, Christ proclaimed His victory over Satan by making a public display—the cross. In that one powerful action Jesus brought the ruler of this world to shame and subdued him.

Victory in Jesus

We don't have to pray for that kind of victory in the future. We already have it! God gave it to us two thousand years ago, when Jesus shouted, "It is finished," from the cross. As Paul could say, "In all of these things, we are more than superconquerors through him who loved us and gave himself for us" (*see* Romans 8:37).

How Big a Victory?

More than that, Paul says in 2 Corinthians 2:14 (NAS): ". . . Thanks be to God, who always leads us in His triumph in Christ, and manifests through us the sweet aroma of the knowledge of Him in every place." Notice those words *always* and *every place*.

How big is this victory? What kind does He promise? Not a *sometimes* victory or one that happens when everything is just right—an *always* and *every place* victory. The first word speaks of time, the second one of space. That covers all the bases.

Jesus has the power and ability to give you the victory, but you have to respond to it. At first, some people have the idea that being a Christian should exclude them from having troubles. "I had a lot of troubles before I met the Lord," they say. "But I expected that when I became a Christian, they'd all disappear." That's just not true. You will have trials regardless, and anyone who tells you otherwise is mistaken. But God still provides victory in the midst of troubles.

The victorious life does not mean God removes the problems, but that He gives you power to meet them. "Is that possible?" you ask. Paul says so: "We are afflicted in every way, but not crushed; perplexed, but not despairing; persecuted, but not forsaken; struck down, but not destroyed" (2 Corinthians 4:8 NAS).

In this verse Paul compared the believer to a wrestler. "You are pressed in every way, but not pinned." Got the picture? "I'm like a wrestler whose opponent has thrown him to the canvas," he says. "Yes, I've been flattened, but the devil can't pin my shoulders."

Maybe you feel "pressed down." You've lost your job and can't find another. Financially you're stressed, but Satan can't pin you. Or perhaps you have a marriage that has gone sour, and you wonder if it's even worth getting up off the canvas; but the enemy can't get the victory. "We are pressed in every way," says Paul, "but not pinned."

When Paul says we can be "perplexed, but not despairing," the original language means "boxed in, hemmed in." Like a halfback who takes the pitchout, going to the right, and sees no openings, he reverses his field, only to find that, too, hopeless. He can't get away—no holes, nothing but opponents poised to tackle him. Though Paul's boxed in, God says, "You can be that way, but I'll provide a way out." You, too, can escape!

As a runner you line up for a race, the gun sounds, and you fire out, but soon you are out of breath. You begin to have cramps, and the others pull away from you. You say to yourself, *I can't even finish the race.* But before you give up and drop out, listen to what Paul says: "Persecuted but not forsaken." Though you fall behind and never lead the pack, you *will* finish the race. Even if you don't come in first or second, you will win a victory.

Finally, Paul says we are "struck down, but not destroyed." Like a boxer, you can be knocked down, but the devil can't knock you out. Why? Because a Christian has victory always and in every place.

The Fragrance of Victory

"But thanks be to God, who always leads us in His triumph in Christ, and manifests through us the sweet aroma [sweet perfume] of the knowledge of Him in every place. For we are a fragrance of Christ to God among those who are being saved and among those who are perishing; to the one an aroma from death to death, to the other an aroma from life to life . . ." (2 Corinthians 2:14–16 NAS).

How was such victory perfume made in the first century A.D.? Herbs were crushed and burned as incense. Up and down the streets the priests paraded, swinging incense pots, and you could smell the sweet aroma for miles.

Long before the general appeared, the people could smell that aroma. Today they ought to be able to smell it when you walk into your office or your home or when they see your marriage. Let others smell the sweet perfume of Jesus Christ in your life and church.

Recently I saw an advertisement for a new resort. It read, "The Right Time, the Right Place." *That sure would be great,* I thought. *If only we did find ourselves there all the time.* How much more often we find ourselves at the wrong time and in the wrong place.

Acts 16 shows Paul at the wrong time—midnight—in the wrong place—jail. False accusations had caused Paul and Silas to be thrown there, the magistrates had them beaten just for good measure. Nothing of the Christian fragrance filled the prison, just a stale, foul odor.

Once they had been beaten, the jailer jammed them into the stocks. How did they respond? Rather than complaining about the pain or giving up, the two men remembered the *every-place* promise of God and that they were down, but not out. They praised God, regardless! Even if they didn't feel much like it at first, that changed, because soon the Holy Spirit came upon them. If you sniff the air, you smell something more than the rotten odor of prison. You can catch a whiff of the sweet aroma of victory! The jailer, his family, and all the other inmates in essence said. "We have never smelled anything like that. We want it, too." They all joined the victory parade.

At first the pagan jailer turned to what he thought was his only option: suicide! Because he did not know God, he began to fall into the negative trap.

Victory for Whom?

Praising in the face of problems only works for Christians (those who love the Lord, as described in Romans 8:28). God does not make everything work for good for unbelievers. In fact He may choose to have their lives fall apart, so that they will turn to Him. Look at what happened to that jailer, whose life had to be in the balance before he could accept Christ.

Also everything may not work for good when believers gripe and complain. Look at the Israelites who wandered in the desert for forty years. They complained, "We're all going to die. We had it better in Egypt."

God said, "Whatever my ears hear them say, that will I do to them."

The Israelites whined, "We're all going to die." So they did. The next words in this passage (*see* Numbers 14:28, 29) are: "And their carcasses shall fall in the wilderness." The very words of their murmuring came true. They never saw the Promised Land because they couldn't stop complaining.

By the same token, God loves and favors those who exercise their faith. If you thank God when you don't feel thankful, you fulfill the conditions of Romans 8:28.

When the Roof Caves In

When you face trials and troubles in your life, remember what you have read here, but even more, put it into practice!

In the 1952 Olympics a young Hungarian looked down his pistol barrel and hit the bull's-eye again and again. He just couldn't miss. With his perfect right-hand-and-eye coordination, he won a gold medal. Six months later, he lost his right arm in an accident. But in Melbourne, four years later, he returned, to hit the bull's-eye again and again, this time with his left hand. Because he chose not to be limited by his handicap, he won a second gold medal.

For that champion, necessity was the author of change. Out of necessity, he achieved a great victory. It can be so in your life, too. Make the hardships that come upon you turn into stepping-stones that help you cross to new shores of achievement. Learn to win when the roof caves in!